THE CHRISTIAN AFTER DEATH

THE CHRISTIAN AFTER DEATH

BY

ROBERT ERVIN HOUGH, D.D.
Pastor, Central Presbyterian Church
Jackson, Mississippi

MOODY PRESS
CHICAGO

THE CHRISTIAN AFTER DEATH

Printed in the United States of America

TABLE OF CONTENTS

Chapter I

WHAT IS DEATH?

Death is universally regarded as a "fearful thing." Everywhere and in every age man fears death. One of the oldest writers of the world describes it as a land of darkness where the light itself is as darkness. Such manifestation of fear comes not from the lowest order of life only but from the highest human nature. This is perhaps the last fear that is overcome in the heart of the trusting saint. There is no experience of life so generally dreaded as death, and there is no topic about which people are so reticent to speak as death.

The Chinese people have long been taught by dark superstition that to name any evil condition or circumstance, however casually, is to invite that evil thing to befall the one who speaks of it. Hence, their custom is to evade using in conversation any word significant of pain, disease, accident, death, or other misfortune. In place of such terms, they employ roundabout and obscure allusions.

People may deny any tendency toward such a superstition; nevertheless, they try to evade thinking or talking about death, lest in so doing they bring it nearer. All know well how inevitable is their approaching farewell to earth; but none-the-less they cultivate the delusive habit which implies that they can postpone what they ignore, and divest all terror from what they persist in forgetting. That is a dangerous position to assume.

It has been well said that life can never mean as much to those who stubbornly turn their backs on death as to those who frankly face it and learn to understand something of what it is and what it does to them.

From all available records there have been only two persons to go from earth without passing through the experience of death. These two were Enoch, "the seventh from Adam"; and Elijah, the fearless and uncompromising prophet of Jehovah who lived and labored in the olden lays of Israel's history in the land of promise. Nothing is recorded of Enoch save that he "walked with God: and he was not; for God took him" (Gen. 5:24); and that he prophesied concerning the coming of the Lord to execute judgment upon the ungodly (Jude 14, 15). There is not one word since his passing concerning his present state. But on the other hand, much is written concerning Elijah. Of him it was prophesied that he would return before the coming of the great and dreadful day of the Lord (Mal. 4:5, 6). And when John the Baptist began his ministry in the wilderness of Judea, it was thought that he was Elijah risen from the dead. But John steadfastly denied that he was Elijah. And a little later Elijah did appear in person on earth and was seen by men. When the Lord was transfigured on the mount, Elijah was one of the witnesses of that marvelous event; he was recognized by Peter, who wanted to build a tabernacle for him, as well as one each for the Lord and for Moses. The two heavenly visitants were representatives; Moses, of those who pass through death, and Elijah, of those who will not pass through it. Not everyone will sleep (that is, die), but those who do not die will be changed, in a moment, in the twinkling of an eye (I Cor. 15:51, 52).

It is estimated that there are more than two billion people living in the world today. In fifty years most of these will have gone from earth. In a hundred years only a little handful will be left, and these only for a few more days. It will be written of them that they have died, and the roll of the dead begun in Genesis, the fifth chapter, will be enlarged by the addition of another generation.

Since death is an experience which none will likely escape, it behooves everyone to learn all he can about it in order to be prepared to meet it when it comes. There are of course various opinions among men concerning death. Lecky describes death as "the melancholy anticlimax to life," and many share with him this conception. Death appears to those who entertain this view as a terrible contradiction of man's destiny, the blasting of all his hopes, and the ending of his brief experience as a human being —a terrible enemy to contemplate.

To some, death is purely a natural event; it belongs to this life as do many other experiences. It is a part of the process of living, for which man is no more responsible than for his birth. And as such, he need concern himself no more about it than about other matters pertaining to life here.

To others, death is regarded as a gracious intervention to remove one out of the distressing experiences which cannot be disposed of in any other way. It comes to relieve the aged of their infirmities, the weak, the weary, and the worn of these unbearable ills of life.

But there is far more to man's death than the working out of natural law. Death is infinitely more than the natural and inevitable breaking down of man as he is now constituted. Death reaches immeasurably beyond the mere consummation of man's existence here. To think of death as being no more than physical dissolution is to share the pagan view that man is no more than an offspring from the animal and falls under the same law of death. But when man appeared on the earth, he was as something new in the world of life. Here was a rational and an accountable being made in the "image of God"; a creature come to dwell on earth, capable of an entirely different kind of life from that of the animal creation and with great possibilities of progress and happiness. He bore in himself the evidence that he was created for a destiny unlike that of all other creatures, a destiny to be fully realized only in eternity.

The Scripture uses the term *death* in a number of ways. There is a death which relates to man's physical nature, that is, of his body. Then there is spiritual death, which relates to man's natural state in relation to God. The natural, the unregenerate man, is described as "dead in trespasses and sins"; he is "without Christ"; being an alien from the commonwealth of Israel, and a stranger from the covenants of promise, "having no hope, and without God in the world" (Eph. 2:12). There is, then, a living existence that is called "death," or a death in life which is not a cessation of being, but a continuation of living existence in alienation from its Creator, and in rebellion against Him. Death, in a spiritual sense, is a state and condition in the same way that spiritual life is a state and condition. The Lord said, "This is life eternal, that they might know thee, the only true God and Jesus Christ whom thou hast sent." In contrast with the spiritual life, there is also spiritual death, which takes place prior to the death of the body. Spiritual death may reign while the natural life continues. "I know thy works, that thou hast a name that thou livest, and art dead" (Rev. 3:1). This is what is meant by being "dead in trespasses and sins," for, "to be carnally minded is death, but to be spiritually minded is life and peace." Therefore, the "wages of sin" is the continuation of spiritual death, which is separation from God, the Author and Source of life. "God is not the God of the dead but of the living." Thus death holds sway, even while the man is naturally alive in all his faculties.

Again, the word *death* is used in a figurative or secondary sense. The prodigal son is described by his father as "dead," when in reality he was only in a "far country," and away from home. Paul, also, described the pleasure-loving and pleasure-seeking woman as dead while she liveth (I Tim. 5:6). The term *death* is likewise used to describe the eternal state of the wicked, which is called "the second death." It does not mean destruction, annihilation, or cessation of being; but life that is estranged from God, a life that is lost forever in a world of darkness. It is *second* relatively to the preceding physical death of the wicked in unbelief and rejection of God. That the second death is not annihilation is shown by a comparison of Revelation 19:20 with Revelation 20:10. After one thousand years in the lake of fire, the beast and the false prophet are still there, undestroyed.

While each of the various usages of the word *death* seem to convey a different meaning, the central idea in each instance is the same. Its basic meaning is *separation* from life or from something that is most desirable.

It is physical death, however, that is to be the primary subject of this study, that is, death as it relates to the body as presently constituted. This is the death usually thought of when the subject is mentioned. And it is the one people most dread, if they dread any. As another has pointed out, with a good deal of force, most people do not *fear* death; they simply *ignore* it. While they cannot forget that death is in the world, since every funeral reminds them of it, they practically regard themselves as immortal. This attitude toward death was never truer than of this present age, which hates meditation, especially on disagreeable subjects. At least until the war, it was too much, "act, act in the living present," as if there were no future worth considering. Probably it is true that much of the weakness of the Christian life of today results from this one-sided insistence on present duties and the absolute ignoring of future rewards and punishment, and even so potent and arresting a fact as death itself.

What then is physical death? It is the separation for the time being of the soul from the body. This is an experience which men dread, and rightly so, for it does mean much for one to pass from all he knows to the unknown land—to cast off all moorings, and set forth upon an uncharted ocean, bound for a port which he has never visited, and from which he has met no returning visitor. If there are any stirrings of curiosity left in one after the siftings of the world, he should await the journey with desire to know what lies beyond. And if he is prudent, he will endeavor to prepare himself for the true land of his heart's desire by speaking its language here and practicing its ways like the expectant traveler who learns beforehand something of the tongue and manners of the land to which he intends to go. The land to which he goes is to be his eternal home.

Physical death is the final breakdown of the body, which the Psalmist describes as fearfully and wonderfully made; it is the total disintegration of this marvelous structure. And let it not be forgotten that it is only the body that dies. Its elements have only returned, for a time, to that state in which they existed before a spirit sent from God took them into a strange partnership which will never be completely and finally broken. It is the dissolving of our earthly house of this tabernacle, from which "we are willing rather to be absent" in order "to be present with the Lord."

Death seems to end all, but in reality it ends nothing. It does not even break the continuity of life. At best it is only an incident in the great program of living. And the separation between body and soul for a time really makes but little difference so far as the essential man is concerned. The Lord, by His own death, has robbed death of its sting and the grave of its victory. Hence, while death can destroy for a little while the house in which the person lives, it must leave untouched the life, the mind, the soul, the spirit—the person himself. By the Lord's death, death is forever destroyed, brought to nought, forever eliminated from life, "made of none effect." His death has changed the whole meaning of death for the believer. Instead of being the dreaded door into oblivion, it has been transformed into the gate of life, through which the Christian enters upon the full fruition of all the blessed things for which he has longed. It ushers in the perfect life, and makes possible the perfect service. Left alone, the death of the body would have been sealed in eternal death. But Christ Jesus came for the express purpose of destroying death. And this He did by dying. He thereby brought life and immortality to light through the gospel (II Tim. 1:10). It was not man who got the victory over death; death got the victory over man. Man did not, nor can he alone, overcome death. Jesus Christ the Lord did that for believers. They get the victory through the Lord Jesus Christ alone. "Thanks be unto God which giveth us the victory through our Lord Jesus Christ." As someone has said, "For the believer, death was 'destroyed' *de jure* at the cross, and will be 'abolished' *de facto* in the glory." The last enemy to be destroyed is death.

The word "abolish" means to render idle, inactive, inoperative, to deprive of strength (I Cor. 15:26). Christ abolished death by introducing man to spiritual life, so that physical death is no longer a penalty, but is henceforth "but the gateway of life immortal" (see John 11:26). In His own personal resurrection the Lord abolished death. The stone was rolled away, not to permit Him to come out, but to show that He was no longer there; and since that is true, the believer is not looking for death; he is looking for Him who triumphed over death. Death still exists, but it no longer "reigns" over man (Rom. 5:14-17). And even as a physical fact, its abolition is decreed, "the last enemy to be destroyed is death" (I Cor. 15:26).

There is much to be learned about death from the Word of God. But even after learning all that may now be known, doubtless there will be much that remains to be learned. But one can well afford to wait, content with what God has been pleased to reveal. It is enough to know that Jesus Christ the Lord, that great Shepherd of the sheep, went this way before His followers. And He goes this way still, as the personal Friend and Helper of all His true disciples when they walk in the "valley of the shadow" of death; and since that is true the believer can sing triumphantly, "Yea, though I walk through the valley of the shadow of death, I will fear no evil; for thou art with me; thy rod and thy staff they comfort me."

There are two ways of looking at death—two standpoints from which to view it. Surveyed from nature's point of view, death is much to be dreaded. It is man's last enemy, his most terrible foe. There is nothing which individuals possess that death will not take from them—riches, honors, dignities, pleasures—all, in short, that the human heart values—all that goes to make up the sum of human happiness in this world. Everything that man possesses here must pass away under the withering touch of the hand of death, and what a person might have been becomes a thing of the past. The opportunities of which one does not take advantage pass into the yesterday of his life. Warnings which came to him, and which he did not heed, will face him as he comes to the time of reckoning. The wealth, the honor, the splendor of this world cannot purchase one moment's respite from the cruel grasp of the king of terror. When death comes, all must go. It comes as the great thief to kill and to destroy.

But there is another way of looking at death. It is from the standpoint of the believer. In I Corinthians 3:22, there is a most unusual item set down in that marvelous inventory of the believer's possessions. "All are yours," says the apostle, and among the "all," he puts "death." Think of this! What a strange possession! "Death is yours." How can this be? How has it come to pass that man's last enemy, his most dreaded foe, that from which he shrinks with such horror, this terrible thing called death, should actually be an item in the Christian's possession?

The cross furnishes the answer. Christ died, the Just for the unjust, according to the Scriptures, for the believer's sins. Thus He has taken the sting from death, for the sting of death is sin; and He has not only removed the sting but has completely changed the character of death for the believer.

Speaking of the sting of death reminds one of the story which Dr. James M. Gray used to tell to illustrate the removal of that sting. One summer day, a farmer was stung by a bee. Dr. Gray visited him at the time, and he told him about the incident. "Well," said the farmer, "there is one thing that brings me a good deal of satisfaction anyway; that bee will never sting another man!" "Why," asked his visitor, "did you kill it?" "No," said he, "but do you not know that a bee has only one sting, and when it stings a man, it leaves the sting in him?" Death has but one sting, and that one was lodged in the body of Christ on the cross. And since that is true, death may alight upon the believer, but there is no sting in it for him. Its power to torment is gone. Death is no longer the jailer of the grave, but the porter that opens the gate of paradise.

Thus it is that death is the Christian's possession. What a marvelous change! Viewed from nature's standpoint, man belongs to death; but from faith's standpoint, death belongs to man. In the old creation there is not so much as a single thing which death does not take from man; in the new creation, on the contrary, there is not a single thing which death does not give to him. There is not a privilege, not a blessing, not a dignity, which he possesses as a Christian that he does not owe to death. He has life through death; forgiveness of sins through death; everlasting righteousness through death; eternal glory through death—all through the precious death of Christ.

Glorious fact! Death belongs to the Christian. Since that is true, should he any longer fear it? Surely not, for its character is so completely changed that if it should come to him, it could do him only the very best service; namely, to dissolve his connection with all that is mortal; to snap the link that binds him to scenes of sorrow and trial; to deliver him from a world of sin and wickedness, and introduce him to a scene of ineffable bliss, holy repose, and unbroken communion.

CHAPTER II

WILL THE DEAD LIVE AGAIN?

IN THE LONG AGO the patriarch Job asked, "If a man die, shall he live again?" This is still the question for which the human heart anxiously desires to have a satisfactory answer. For loved ones are continually slipping away into the land from which no traveler returns; and as the bereaved gaze into the darkness after their dear ones, their troubled hearts constantly repeat this age-old question, "Have they ceased to be? If not, where are they now, and how do they fare?"

There are three general answers given. There is the answer which the scientist offers. He says, "There may be a future life; I know nothing from the constitution of the universe as it is understood, which forbids it." There is the answer of the philosopher which declares, "There ought to be a future life; everything I know demands it." And, of course, there is the answer which divine revelation gives.

As to the *body,* the Scripture teaches that it returns to the earth from whence it came. "For dust thou art, and unto dust shalt thou return," is the divine fiat (Gen. 3:19). And man has no difficulty in discovering that this very thing happens to it. The body is dead; it refuses to function; it becomes cold and lifeless, and soon ceases to exist in any form. Realizing that the body is dead, and will remain so, loving hands take it up and tenderly lay it away in "the city of the dead," where it sleeps its last long sleep.

As far back as history records, special effort has been made to preserve the body from disintegration, but without success. Magnificent mausoleums are erected at fabulous cost for the purpose of preserving it from decay, at least as long as possible. The ancient Egyptians developed a method of embalming the body, and so efficient did they become in this art that bodies buried for centuries have been found in an almost perfect state of preservation. But even so, the body was still lifeless. All that man can do either to prevent death from doing its work, or to rescue the body from its clutches after it has claimed its victim, is futile.

But what becomes of the *soul* after death? Does it die also? Some claim that it does, that it has no more life after separation from the body than does the body itself. And they try to persuade men that they are altogether material with a bit of breath in their nostrils; to believe that as a candle goes out when burned to the socket, so they, when the breath of life ceases, are forever extinguished. According to this view, death ends all existence for either the soul or body. And strange as it may seem, those who advocate this theory claim scriptural support for it. The book of the Bible upon which they rely chiefly to prove their case is Ecclesiastes. And from it they take such passages as these: "For that which befalleth the sons of men befalleth beasts; even one thing befalleth them: as the one dieth, so dieth the other; yea, they have all one breath; so that a man hath no preëminence above a beast; for all is vanity" (Eccles. 3:19); "All things come alike to all: there is one event to the righteous, and to the wicked; . . . they go to the dead" (Eccles. 9:2, 3). It is admitted that from a superficial reading of these passages, they do appear to support the argument that man's existence ends with death. But those who cite them as proof-texts disregard two important facts.

First, they fail to take into consideration the *purpose* for which the book was written. It is the conclusion of the wisest man who gave himself to the task of discovering the secrets of life apart from revelation. At the beginning of his reign, Solomon, the human author of the book, was granted the privilege of asking God for whatever he might desire, to insure the greatness of his reign as the successor of his father David, the great and good king of Israel. Realizing something of his utter inability to meet the weighty responsibilities of this high office, he besought the Lord to give him "an understanding heart" to judge the people, and to discern between good and bad (I Kings 3:5-15). God was so pleased with his request that He granted Solomon an unusual degree of wisdom and knowledge. And in granting him this great gift, God said to him, "There was none like thee before thee, neither after thee shall any arise like unto thee" (I Kings 3:12). And until this day Solomon is regarded as the wisest man who ever lived.

With this extraordinary supply and quality of wisdom, Solomon set himself to the task of considering "all things that are done under the sun," and recording his findings in a book. The result of this investigation is the Book of

Ecclesiastes. According to his own statement, he purposely limits his record to what he was able to discover for himself "under the sun," and arrives at his conclusions by observing exclusively things from the earth level. In all of his investigation he never looks at things *above* the sun, but only at those *under* the sun. The book, therefore, must be regarded as containing the verdict of the natural man at his highest point in wisdom and understanding; and some of its conclusions are wholly apart from divine revelation.

And what is the conclusion of Solomon as he attempts to answer this question by his own wisdom and research? It is this: when a man dies and is buried, so far as man can see, that is the end of his existence. Man cannot see beyond the grave; and apart from the teaching of God's Word knows nothing of what lies beyond that little mound of earth. And so it comes to this, that Solomon with all his wisdom and with every facility for conducting such a research, discovers he cannot find any evidence under the sun of existence after death. Hence all the Book of Ecclesiastes purports to do is to set down for man's information this conclusion. That this is a true statement of the purpose of the book is evident from Solomon's declaration: "And I gave my heart to seek and search out by wisdom concerning all things that are done under heaven: . . . I have seen all the works that are done under the sun; and, behold, all is vanity and vexation of spirit" (Eccles. 1:13, 14). And should the wisest man today attempt a similar investigation apart from all knowledge of divine revelation, he would arrive at the same conclusion. But the fact that man cannot see beyond the grave does not prove there is no life beyond it. It merely reveals the limitation of man's knowledge, and his abiding need of divine guidance.

The second fact disregarded by those who would use this book to prove the non-existence of man after death is that *it concludes with the expressed conviction that there is life after death*: "Then shall the dust return to the earth as it was: and the spirit shall return unto God who gave it" (Eccles. 12:7).

To declare that this present life is all there is for man, or even the highest form of life, is to deny the teaching of God's Word, and practically to charge that since the whole creation is groaning in pain and dying and nothing attains perfection here, God made a mistake in creating anything. But God made no mistake. The answer for the failures of this life is a future life where man will have the proper environment and opportunity to realize fully the greater hope and aspirations of his soul which can never be brought to fruition here, because of the effects of his own sin and the limited time in which he has to work.

Now in striking contrast to human reasoning, the Bible teaches with all definiteness that when the soul is separated from the body, life does not become extinct, or lose its personal continuity; for personal continuity and life in the body are not identical, the one does not depend upon the other. While it is true that the spirit of life is necessary for existence on earth, it is not true that personality may not, and does not, continue to exist in another form after death. If man is not to live after death, then it is not eternal life which Christ gives His followers; and the eternal keeping which He promises those to whom this life is imparted is a delusion. In all His teachings Christ nowhere intimated that death is an eternal sleep; but on the contrary, He always held out the highest hope for the future to all His followers. What could be more definite and reassuring, for instance, than this promise: "My sheep hear my voice, and I know them, and they follow me: and I give unto them eternal life; and they shall never perish, neither shall any man pluck them out of my hand" (John 10:27, 28)?

During the days of His public ministry, Christ used a number of terms to describe death; but not one of them, even in the most remote way, suggested extinction. For example, word came to Him one day that Lazarus was dead, and in announcing it to His disciples He did not use the word "death," but said very simply, "Our friend Lazarus sleepeth; but I go, that I may awake him out of sleep" (John 11:11). Sleep is not death: it is not the cessation of being. On another occasion He spoke of His own departure as "going to the Father," and promised that those who accept Him as Saviour would also go to be with Him there (John 14:1-28). In these declarations there is nothing that suggests death is the end of existence either for Christ or the believer. On the mount of transfiguration Christ is seen in conversation with two men, Moses and Elijah, both of whom had passed from this life centuries before. If passing from this life means extinction, then how could these men be present on this occasion? These incidents, along with many others which might be cited, not only refute the idea of extinction, but also allow no gap or break in one's existence.

Furthermore, Christ taught that men were not to seek their permanent good here, but were to sacrifice even that which was pleasant and agreeable for the sake of better things to come. He went so far as to promise to prepare a place for them, and to come again and receive them unto Himself. In all this there is nothing but assurance of a glorious future life.

In addition to what has been said, the conceptions and experiences of believers down the ages in regard to death also should be considered. What did they think about life beyond? And how did they behave themselves in view of that life? In the Book of Genesis, the fifth chapter, there is a very remarkable record. It is about Enoch, who walked with God, and how God took him to be with Him. But that is not all that is known of Enoch. Jude says that he was a prophet, and that one of the subjects of his prophecy was the coming of the Lord with His saints with Him, a mighty host of them. This prophecy clearly shows that Enoch, the man who was close enough to God to walk with Him for three hundred years, believed the saints are in existence in spite of their death, or they could not come with Christ. And as for Enoch himself, evidently he is living somewhere today; for God took him and did not let him die.

Then there is a most illuminating chapter about the patriarchs in the letter to the Hebrews, the eleventh chapter. There it is told how these men and women journeyed through life with the assurance of future life burning brightly in their souls. And so thoroughly convinced were they of future existence in a higher sphere they described themselves as "strangers and pilgrims on the earth." When the king of Egypt, evidently impressed by the great age of Jacob, inquired as to his age, he replied: "The days of the years of my pilgrimage are one hundred and thirty years; few and evil have the days of the years of my life been, and I have not attained unto the days of the years of my fathers in the days of their pilgrimage." This confession of being a stranger was not drawn from the patriarch by his feeling of the shortness of life, for he considered his fathers who had reached a much greater age as pilgrims also; but from the conviction that he would continue to live after death in a better world. Nor did this conception of life as a pilgrimage arise from the fact that, as in the case of some of them, they had to live their lives away from their kindred and from the graves of their ancestors; for it is distinctly recorded that if they had desired an earthly fatherland they had ample opportunity to return to find their kindred, and to live again among the traditions of their fathers.

But the idea of an earthly heritage was not in their minds when they described themselves as pilgrims and strangers longing for a home. The longing was a spiritual one and continued as long as they lived. Thus they recognized God as their portion; and in turn, He was not ashamed to be called their God. And since God is the God of the living and not of the dead, these pilgrims are not dead; they are still living, and are dwellers in the land which He has prepared for them.

Note should be taken also of the character of the city these pilgrims were expecting. It was not to be a temporary, makeshift sort of habitation. It was a "city which hath foundations, whose builder and maker is God" (Heb. 11:10). They had been accustomed to the tent life and as they moved from one pasturage to another, it was with the full assurance that when their pilgrimage ended here a more glorious habitation beyond their fondest dreams awaited them. And it is to be a better country not simply because it promises a greater amount of material blessing, or more lasting good, such as the earth gives for a few years; but because it lays before the pilgrim's hope another kind of good, as different from the earthly as it is possible to be. So the tent dweller traveled on with his desires on a new object, on the heavenly inheritance which comprises all that is holy and truly blessed. These pilgrims had an abiding faith in God, and believed that since God was not ashamed to be called their God, He would take care of their interests by bringing to pass the full realization of their holy desire to be with God in that heavenly city. Is it possible to conceive that God will be ashamed of such hearts that breathed toward Him the new language of love and confidence? Even if He had made no promise, could He forbear to show them His complacency in their choice? Since He has made them promises both great and precious, it is inconceivable that He will fail in the fulfillment of them. Will He not value such faith, such longing after Him, such surrender of their happiness into His hands, too much to disappoint such confidence? And since He has prepared for them a city, His preparation will be as large as their hopes. What He has prepared for them is said to be a city, something abiding and stationary, in contrast with this temporary and uncertain state of existence. The thought of a city seemed to these tent dwellers an emblem of what was lasting and secure. They lived in tents and tabernacles in this world, and not only did not want a permanent abiding place here, but felt they could find none. Still, they longed for something abiding; for death, decay, change, and uncertainty are alien to man's nature, and run counter to his inner longing for immortality, which God will satisfy in His own good way and time.

There is yet another statement in the Scripture concerning these patriarchs which clearly indicates belief in the future life. It is said of many of them, when they passed out of this life, they were gathered to their fathers (Judg. 2:10; II Kings 22:20). This does not mean they are buried in or near the graves of their fathers. Abraham, Jacob, Moses, Aaron, and many others of whom the expression is used were buried in graves far remote from the sepulchers of their ancestors; and yet they are said to have been gathered to their fathers. It means far more than the placing of the body near that of those who have gone on ahead. It implies the belief in a definite conscious association with loved ones who had preceded them only a little while to the better world.

Again, there must be a richer and higher life than is ever known here because of the certain feeling of incompleteness of which everyone is more or less conscious. One finds himself following aims and ideals which are quite beyond his reach within the limits of this finite life. There is something in the human soul which stretches over into eternity, and which it will take eternity to satisfy. Dr. Godet said, "Life in the Scriptures denotes a fully satisfied existence in which all the faculties find their fullest exercise and their truest occupation." How did this sense of incompleteness come to be in the soul of man? There are those who claim it is a natural instinct. That may be true, but it is not the explanation for the believer. In discussing the assurance of a future life, Paul says that Christians have "the earnest of the spirit," that is, a kind of pledge wrought within them by God, that they will live a richer and fuller life beyond (II Cor. 5:5).

Is it not clear that life here and now is only one part—a smaller and preparatory part—of a larger life beyond? Nowhere did Christ suggest to men that they were to find their permanent good here; but on the contrary, He spoke about their being persecuted and cast out for His name's sake, and suffering all kinds of privation. He comforted them, however, with the assurance that they would reap a rich reward in the life that is yet to be, and for which this present one is but the vestibule. It is said that when the great Puritan, Owen, lay on his deathbed, his secretary wrote (in his name) to a friend, "I am still in the land of the living." "Stop," said Owen, "alter that, say: 'I am yet in the land of the dying, but I hope soon to be in the land of the living.' "

Eternal life is not life after death. It is the kind of life that is above death, above the influence and power of death. The believer has it now. If he has it not, death will not give it to him or disclose it to him. If he has it, death cannot quench it or take it away.

Chapter III

WHAT GAIN DOES DEATH BRING?

Man continues to live after death. Death does not interrupt life at all, not even for one moment. Only the place of living and the form of life are changed. Nothing is known experimentally either of the place or the kind of life that is to be. But that does not mean that the believer is without instruction concerning it.

As to the present state of the departed saints, various views are entertained. There are those who look upon death as a calamity, as a catastrophe which ends the activities and hopes of men. They regard it as an irreparable loss, and as to what lies beyond, the tendency of this age has been toward agnosticism and skepticism. The fact of death, its inevitability, its uncertainty hang like a dark cloud over the consciousness of men. It is a subject avoided in conversation. Bacon said: "Men fear death as children fear the dark." And Byron wrote: "Oh, God, it is a fearful thing to see the human soul take wing." Even in the church, the Biblical teaching on the subject has been displaced many times by a pagan view of death. It is unfortunate that so many Christians have this gloomy, erroneous conception of death. They have robbed themselves of a great blessing and cast a dark shadow upon the happiness of others.

The conception which the Word of God gives concerning the death of the believer is a different and brighter picture. It is not a catastrophe like a shipwreck in which all possessions are lost and passengers are saved as by the skin of their teeth. It is a gain, a deliverance, a new beginning, an entrance into a larger sphere of life, experience, fellowship, and service.

When it comes to the proof of the type of life on the other side of death, there is very little in the Scripture of a detailed character. God has seen fit to reveal only a few facts in His Word concerning the state of the holy dead; but what He has revealed is very clear and is sufficient to establish the truth in the mind and heart of the believer. In considering this subject, therefore, it behooves men to tread softly, to take no partial view of truth, nor to seek to be wise above what is written, but reverently to gather up every portion of truth as God has graciously given it.

Whatever else may be said concerning the condition of the believer after death, it is certain he is not in a state of unconscious existence. The doctrine sometimes taught today that after death the soul sleeps is not only unscriptural but most dangerous. Though dead to the world and its activities, the departed are not dead to God. Death is not a state of sleep and insensibility. It is a state of recognition and remembrance.

The Christian cannot expect details, for the life beyond is outside his present range of understanding. But there is much that gives a thrilling intimation of what awaits the believer upon receiving his release from this present life. What are some of these intimations? When the Lord was on the mount of transfiguration talking with Moses and Elijah, the subject of their conversation was His decease which He should accomplish at Jerusalem (Luke 9:31). The Greek word for decease is "exodus," the word that describes the deliverance of Israel from Egyptian bondage. Thus the going hence is not into something lower, less desirable, but into something higher and more desirable. Later, Peter uses the same word in reference to his own death (II Peter 1:15). The idea that Moses, Elijah and Peter had, was not that death is loss but gain, a deliverance like that of the Israelites from slavery into freedom.

Paul, in writing to Timothy concerning his own approaching death, employs a happy phrase. He calls is "the time of my departure" (II Tim. 4:6). The word "departure" is a nautical term referring to a ship getting ready to set sail, casting off her shore lines and putting out into the ocean. Paul's idea of death is not a shipwreck, but a ship ready. The ship was built for the open seas, her true element, and to meet the end for which she was designed, she must "depart," cast off the lines which bind her to the shore. A ship is never seen to true advantage unless upon the open sea. There, laden with a rich cargo, with sails set for the breeze, headed on an errand of good will for a foreign port, she is fulfilling the true design of her builder. So was man created for eternity, for the larger life and fellowship beyond his earthly existence. There, and there only, he will fulfill the larger design of his Maker and Redeemer.

As to the gain that comes to the believer at his departure, that is impossible to evaluate at present. There are, however, some illuminating facts revealed in God's Word. Paul declares, for example, the death of the believer is gain in that he is to be immediately with Christ, which is far better than being here. To be with Christ is a suggestive, comprehensive phrase that covers all the gain. It means the believer exchanges earth for Heaven. Paul does not disparage the blessings he received from God during his earthly pilgrimage. But he knows the blessings that lie beyond will be far richer and more glorious than any he has ever known on earth. The believer exchanges time for eternity. Time is a probationary period filled with toils and trials, tears and disappointments. Eternity is a settled state with progress in life and knowledge. It means he exchanges comparative darkness for clear light. As the apostle says, "For now we see through a glass, darkly; but then face to face." It means he exchanges present limited knowledge for a knowledge commensurate with his new state. "Now I know in part; but then shall I know even as also I am known" (I Cor. 13:12).

Death is gain in that it brings ultimate deliverance from the old Adamic nature. Regeneration produces many vital changes in the life and state of the believer, but none in the fallen nature. That remains unchangeably evil, and with no hope for improvement (Jer. 17:9; Matt. 15:19; Rom. 7:18). The old nature, being the stronghold of sin, resents bitterly the presence of the new nature which comes to all in regeneration. "For the flesh lusteth against the Spirit, and the Spirit against the flesh: and these are contrary the one to the other" (Gal. 5:17). When the flesh would induce the believer to sin, the Spirit is present to oppose the flesh; to give guidance and strength, and indicate the way of escape so that the believer may be able to bear it (I Cor. 10:13). When the Spirit, on the other hand, would direct the believer into the path of full obedience, the flesh is there to resist the Spirit and prevent, if possible, compliance with His promptings. Failure to understand this truth of the continuing struggle between the flesh and the Spirit has brought untold confusion and distress to multitudes.

The instructed believer, however, finds nothing in the presence and activity of the old nature to bring defeat, or even discouragement. For one thing, he knows the power of the old nature over the child of God has been definitely broken, and he no longer has to obey its behests. He knows that by the grace of God he can *put it off* (Eph. 4:22); *keep it under* (I Cor. 9:27); *reckon it to be dead* (Rom. 6:11); *mortify its members* (Col. 3:5); *make no provision for it* (Rom. 13:14); that he can now walk after the Spirit and not fulfill the lusts of the flesh. He knows that by doing these things the impulses of the fallen nature will never be brought to fulfillment in action in his experience. And he knows, beyond all this, that when death comes to release him from the life he now lives in the flesh (Gal. 2:20), he will then have his new nature set free to do God's blessed will perfectly throughout the ceaseless ages of eternity, without let or hindrance. What an inestimable gain that will be! Even the contemplation of such victory thrills the soul with joy.

Death is gain because it brings the believer into the most congenial fellowship and environment. In the present state, no matter how closely one may walk with the Lord, he moves in a sphere where evil is present. He is somewhat like Lot who was vexed with the filthy conversation of the wicked: "For that righteous man dwelling among them, in seeing and hearing, vexed his righteous soul from day to day with their unlawful deeds" (II Peter 2:8). His gain will be separation forever from such contacts. The new society into which he is introduced is selected, protected, and segregated. God Himself is the Lord and Protector of that new state. "And there shall in no wise enter into it any thing that defileth, neither whatsoever worketh abomination, or maketh a lie: but they which are written in the Lamb's book of life" (Rev. 21:27). All who are there will be one in faith, in knowledge, and in confession. They are there, not because of their works, lest they should boast; but because they have washed their robes and made them white in the blood of the Lamb (Rev. 7:14). They are clean in pure surroundings.

Death will bring gain not only in the character but also in the extent of the social contacts. There is a shallow, unscriptural notion that all who die in Christ become angels, and that in Heaven there is only this one class of rational beings. The Word of God tells a different story. The writer to the Hebrews gives an idea of the collective citizenry of the Kingdom of God that lies beyond death. "But ye are come unto mount Sion, and unto the city of the living God, the heavenly Jerusalem, and to an innumerable company of angels, to the general assembly and church of the first-born, which are written in heaven, and to God the Judge of all, and to the spirits of just men made perfect" (Heb. 12:22, 23). This means all will have direct, face-to-face, contact with the redeemed of all ages and with the innumerable holy beings who have never fallen, but who have been for ages in the presence of God and doing His service.

There will be gain likewise in the physical state. It will be a change from weakness to power, from mortality to immortality. It will be a change from a natural body, that is, a body subject to the soul, to a spiritual body, a body under the dominion of the spirit (I Cor. 15:35-58). It will be a body that is not subject to weakness, disease and decay, nor to the limitations which circumscribe its activities here. That is gain worthy of contemplation.

But that is not all. The gain lies further in that the believer will find and enjoy there all he properly valued here. There is such a thing as laying up treasures in Heaven where neither moth nor rust corrupt, and where thieves do not break through and steal, and entering upon the full enjoyment of them in Heaven. Just what these treasures are, one may not be able to describe fully. But it is certain all the gracious things which Christ wrought in His followers by His blessed Spirit during their journey here will be preserved for them, and will be enjoyed by them the moment they reach that shining shore. Death will not rob them of their reward, nor take from them those qualities of heart and mind which came to them through their fellowship with Him here. Everything they have ever had of true value they will take with them, for these values are a part of their very being.

The gain consists likewise in being placed in an irrevocable state. The condition of the departed, though not final in degree, is fixed as to character. Unlike Eden, it is a state incapable of being changed into another less desirable. Sin and death will never be permitted to enter the abode of the sainted dead to disturb their happy lives or to deprive them of their blessed and eternal dwelling place.

Hence, the Scripture dispels any hesitating doubt of the possibility of the believer rejoicing in the glory of God in his disembodied state. One is not to think that the spirit of man which is in him will evaporate when the earthly house dissolves, or that the soul falls asleep and remains in an unconscious existence. No! "The souls of believers do at their death immediately pass into glory" (Westminster Catechism) where they are to be with Christ forever. Is this not what Christ asked of the Father for them when He prayed, "Father, I will that they also, whom thou hast given me, be with me where I am; that they may behold my glory, which thou hast given me" (John 17:24)? And not only will they be with Him immediately, but with Him forever.

Not spilled like water on the ground;
 Not wrapped in dreamless sleep profound;
Not wandering in unknown despair
 Beyond Thy voice, Thine arm, Thy care.
Not left to lie like fallen tree;
 Not dead—but living unto Thee.

It is important to remember, therefore, that the future life is not a mere survival of life, but a quality of life which believers are to find here and practice now, that they may grow from image to image in the likeness of Christ. Death is the soul's emancipation. It is not the riveting of chains, but the breaking of them. It is not the setting of the sun, but the dawn of a new eternal day. It is not the end of the stream, but the fountain flowing into its rightful channel. It is not the ship dropping down into the haven, but the spreading of the sails for the great transoceanic voyage. It is not the winding up of all living, but the beginning of life in all its fullness.

Robert Burdette, in a personal letter shortly before his death, describes how he felt about this voyage:

> I watch the sunset as I look out over the rim of the blue Pacific, and there is no mystery beyond the horizon line, because I know what there is over there. I have been there. I have journeyed in those lands. Over there where the sun is just sinking is Japan. That star is rising over China. In that direction lie the Philippines. I know all that.
>
> Well, there is another land that I look forward to as I watch the sunset. I have never seen it. I have never seen anyone who has been there, but it has a more abiding reality than any of these lands which I do know. This land beyond the sunset—this land of immortality, this fair and blessed country of the soul—why, this Heaven of ours is the one thing in the world which I know with absolute, unshaken, unchangeable certainty. This I know with a knowledge that is never shadowed by a passing doubt. I may not always be certain about this world; my geographical locations may sometimes become confused, but the other—that I know. And as the afternoon sun sinks lower, faith shines more clearly and hope, lifting her voice in a higher key, sings the songs of fruition. My work is about ended, I think. The best of it I have done poorly; any of it I might have done better, but I have done it. And in a fairer land, with finer materials and a better working light, I shall do a better work.

What more do the Father's children need to know about that blessed state? He has given sufficient information to make it most desirable, and it will surely surpass all expectations.

To the saints of God, death is nothing to cause distress or sorrow or fear; for while it does take the saints from things held dear, it brings them into an ever more precious relationship. It makes possible the full enjoyment of the "unsearchable riches of Christ" which are now known only in part. Man made in the image of God and after His likeness, was never meant to walk the earth with aimless feet as if the present life were an end in itself, but rather to press forward with steady footsteps toward the life everlasting. The believer can praise God that his vision of life is not bound by the confines of earth, but enters within the veil where Christ has gone. The unbeliever can see nothing but a black and silent eternity; but the believer, with the eye of faith, sees the fair land that is far off, and sees death as the supreme moment of a new birth for the enthralled soul—the introduction to a new era of life, compared with which the present one is not worthy to be mentioned. Thus, an aged saint, on being reminded of his infirmities, triumphantly declared:

Gone, they tell me is youth,
Gone the strength of my life,
Nothing remains but decline,
Nothing but age and decay.

Not so! I am God's little child,
Only beginning to live.
Coming the days of my prime.
Coming the strength of my life,
Coming the vision of God,
Coming my bloom and my power!

Have you that clear, strengthening, hopeful vision of the eternal world?

CHAPTER IV

WHERE DO THE SPIRITS OF JUST MEN GO AT DEATH?

SINCE THE PERSON himself lives on in conscious awareness after his experience of physical death, there must be some suitable place in which he is to live. He is not a wraith, a mere spectre floating about in space, but is localized somewhat after the fashion of his bodily existence.

Where is that place? Of course there has been a good deal of speculation, both as to its location and character. But like the other questions relating to life, there is no light on the subject apart from divine revelation. A person is limited to God's Word for all the information he has or can hope to have of this life. Unless he has given attention to the matter he may suppose there is not very much said about it in the Scripture. The body of truth revealed on the subject does not bulk very large; but to the earnest seeker after the truth it is exceedingly interesting and satisfying. An examination of what is revealed shows that far more is written than appears to the casual reader.

In seeking for the answer to the question, "Where do the souls of just men go at death?" one should remember that certain changes in the state of the sainted dead were brought about by the death of Christ. And he should likewise bear in mind that the far greater part of the information concerning these changes is contained in that portion of the Word which was written after the death of the Lord; for it was He, through His own death, who "brought life and immortality to light." It would be well to consider some of these changes.

First, Christ's death brought a tremendous change in the character of death. Paul refers very definitely to this change in his second letter to Timothy (1:10), in which he declares that "Christ hath abolished death." Evidently Timothy was somewhat discouraged and alarmed over the future, and the apostle encourages him by assuring him that death, the most dreaded of all enemies, was itself abolished by the death of Christ. Since that event, death has become only an episode, not an end. Death does not and cannot end life. All it can do is to effect a change in the manner and condition of life. The Lord, through His death, deprived death of its strength by introducing the Christian to spiritual life, so that henceforth physical death is no longer a penalty, but the gateway into immortal life. Is this not what Christ meant when He said to Martha in her hour of deepest grief, "Whosoever liveth and believeth in me shall never die"?

It is distinctly said that Christ came to destroy the works of the Devil. What are the works of the Devil? Is not death one of them? for he has "the power of death." The Lord, as the Lamb of God, has borne away the sin of the world; consequently sin can no longer testify against anyone who is united to Christ by faith. Death, being the penalty for sin, and the sin of the believer being taken away through the sacrificial death of Christ, no longer has any claim upon him. If sin is gone, then death is gone; for death "is the wages of sin." When Christ paid the penalty for sin on the cross, death could not hold Him in its power: "He could not be holden of death"; and when He arose in triumph from the grave, at that moment the triumphal course of death was stopped and the triumph of life begun. It is true death still exists, but it no longer "reigns" as it once did over man. Christ has forever triumphed over sin, and consequently over death; and as the believer is in Him by faith, he too has the victory over this last enemy.

Since Christ has completely and gloriously triumphed, the departing believer can now look death squarely in the face and say without the semblance of doubt, "O death, where is thy sting? O grave, where is thy victory? The sting of death is sin; and the strength of sin is the law. But thanks be to God, which giveth us the victory through our Lord Jesus Christ" (I Cor. 15:55-57). No matter what sort of seal is put upon the grave; no matter how deep it may be dug; no matter how absolute may seem the embrace of death, it cannot hold the child of God for a single moment. It can only open the gate of life and let him into the richer and higher life with Christ, which is far better than anything he has ever known, or ever can know in a world of sin and sorrow.

The second thing which Christ accomplished by His death was the change of the abode of the disembodied believer. In the Old Testament several words and figures are used to describe the abode of the righteous. Jacob said, as he was given the blood-stained coat of his son, Joseph, "I will go down into the grave unto my son mourning." In this case the word "grave" means *sheol,* which was not a place of punishment. In the Hebrew language there was one broad word, *sheol,* that described the unseen world to which men go at death. The Greek likewise had a broad word, *hades,* to cover the whole unseen world, both good and bad.

But when the Jews would speak definitely of the abode of the spirits of just men, they would refer to the place as "Abraham's bosom." It was there the righteous went at death, and were at rest and comforted. In the parable of the rich man and Lazarus, it is related that a certain beggar named Lazarus, who was full of sores, was laid at the gate of a certain rich man, desiring to be fed from the crumbs which fell from his bountiful table. But evidently he received little hospitality there. It came to pass the beggar died. Death ended his poverty and suffering. But where did he go when he died? Without any hesitation the Scripture declares that he "was carried by the angels into Abraham's bosom" (Luke 16:22).

At that time, according to the teaching of the Scripture, the place for the departed spirits was divided into two sections. One division of this abode was called "Abraham's bosom" where believers go at death, and the other division was called *"hades,"* the place where the wicked go. Lazarus was carried to Abraham's bosom, where he was comforted, while Dives lifted up his eyes in *hades,* being in torment. There was no passing from the one place to the other; for there was "a great gulf fixed: so that they which would pass from hence to you cannot; neither can they pass to us, that would come from thence" (Luke 16:26).

There are a number of terms in the Scripture used to

describe the abode of the departed until the resurrection of the body and its union again with the spirit. The Saviour informed the dying thief that before the end of the day they would be together in paradise. Paul speaks about going "to be with Christ." Stephen, the first Christian martyr, sees Christ standing at the right hand of God, and he prays Him to receive his spirit. And the Lord on the night in which He was betrayed spoke to His disciples about "my Father's house," and the many mansions which it contained, and of His going to prepare a place for them in it, and of coming again to receive them unto Himself that where He is they may be also.

But some ask, "Is there not confusion in the use of all these terms?" No, there is perfect agreement. Until the ascension of Christ, the righteous went to paradise to *await* His coming; but after His ascension, the believer goes immediately to be with Him.

There are a number of passages of Scripture which make this clear. In Matthew 26:28 these words are found: "For this is my blood of the new testament, which is shed for many for the remission of sins." He is here speaking about His approaching sacrificial death which would be accomplished tomorrow on Calvary's cross. That was done. The blood was shed for the remission of sins as He said it would be. Now put beside this declaration of the Saviour, the passage found in Hebrews 9:22, 24, 28, which reads: "Without shedding of blood is no remission . . . for Christ is not entered into the holy places made with hands, which are the figures of the true; but into heaven itself, now to appear in the presence of God for us. . . . So Christ was once offered to bear the sins of many; and unto them that look for him shall he appear the second time without sin unto salvation." What does this mean? Clearly it means that until the death of Christ there was no taking away of sin, and consequently no one could enter Heaven. What became of the righteous who died before this blood was shed for the remission of sin? The righteous went to paradise, a place of conscious blessing, to await with joyful anticipation the remission of their sin through His atoning sacrifice. Sin was only covered, until atoned for by His death. It was to paradise that the Lord Himself went with the penitent thief when they died on their crosses on Calvary (Luke 23:43).

Third, Christ has abiding authority over *hades* and the grave. In Revelation 1:18, John, the beloved disciple, who was so closely associated with Christ during His earthly life, records a marvelous experience which came to him on the Lord's Day as he was on the Isle of Patmos. He saw Christ; the very Christ whom he had known and loved devotedly on earth; the One who, during the days of His flesh, permitted him to lay his head on His bosom, and ask questions about things which he wished to know. John, moreover, had seen Him die on the cross. He knew full well the story of the crucifixion, having been a witness to it. He knew about His burial, about the care which the Roman government took to prevent any semblance of a resurrection. The tomb was sealed with the great seal of the state, and guarded with a cordon of soldiers; consequently, there was not the slightest chance of any fraud being perpetrated. And now John sees Him again, alive and glorified; the glory is such that John falls at Christ's feet, not in the old familiar way, but as one dead. And as the risen Lord laid His right hand on John and he revived, he noticed two keys in the Lord's hand. The key is the instrument to unlock and release what is confined. What are these keys, and what are their uses? We do not have to speculate, but are plainly told.

One of them is the key to Hell, according to our English translation; but the real significance of the word is *hades,* which means the unseen world—the place of departed human spirits. The Apostles' Creed speaks of Christ descending into "hell," that is to say, into *hades.* It was to this place, *hades,* that Dives and Lazarus went (Luke 16:19-31). But some say that this cannot be, for one man was saved and the other lost. That is true. But you will find, as has already been observed, that this abode was divided into two compartments by a great gulf fixed: one of which was the place of the wicked dead, and the other the place of the righteous. Each went to his own place.

The first key which John sees in Christ's hand is the one with which He unlocked the gate of paradise and set free the mighty host which had been awaiting the hour of His sacrifice that He might lead them triumphantly into Heaven. By this key He liberated the spirits of the righteous—not of the wicked—who had been detained in paradise since the death of righteous Abel, waiting for the shedding of the blood for the remission of sins. "Wherefore he saith, When he ascended up on high, he led captivity captive, and gave gifts unto men. (Now that he ascended, what is it but that he also descended first into the lower parts of the earth? He that descended is the same also that ascended up far above all heavens, that he might fill all things)" (Eph. 4:8-10). So then, according to the teaching of the Scripture, paradise, or as it is expressed in another connection, "Abraham's bosom," was the place of abode of the blessed dead *before* the death of Christ. But since Christ's death the believer goes immediately to be with the Lord and does not pass through the portals of *hades*. That paradise and Heaven are the same today is seen from Paul's vision in which he was caught up to the third heaven, which he identified as paradise (II Cor. 12:2-5).

Then, there is the second key, which is called the key of death, or of the grave. Just as there is a future use of the first key (Rev. 20:13), this key is yet to be used.

There is one other word which needs to be added, and it is this—the present state of the departed believer, while blessed beyond all comprehension, is one of incompleteness. That may shock the reader; for perhaps he has never thought other than that the believers were exactly in the state in which they were to be forever, That idea is true in this respect, that the believers have passed out of the physical and material into the realm of the spiritual and eternal; but they are not yet perfect, nor is their happiness complete. Thinking about it for awhile, one sees that it could not be otherwise. The believer cannot be complete until that body which is an integral part of one's self is renewed and refashioned, and is his again.

Some may object to this fact on the ground that it takes away the joy of Heaven, not only for the Old Testament saints, but for those who go there today. But that is not necessarily true, any more than it limits the enjoyment of the youth to know that he is not yet a man, but that he will be one some day. Does not the very anticipation of manhood add rather than detract from his present joy as a youth?

Not only so, Paul says very definitely that the "unclothed" state is not the highest (II Cor. 5:3, 4). The desire is not to be unclothed, but to be clothed with the house which is from Heaven, so being clothed, the believer will not be found naked.

But while it is a state of incompleteness, in that the body is not yet reunited to the spirit, it is one of indefinable joy. The highest description that can be given of the happiness of the present state is that it is to be with Christ, not in a general sense, but in recognition and fellowship (John 14:3). Since Christ is there and believers are personally associated with Him, no marvel that Paul said he had a desire to depart to be with Christ. It is a state of glorious anticipation. Every saint is there with the full expectation that all the purposes of God will be accomplished. Sin will be banished. Satan's works will be completely and forever destroyed. Death, the last enemy to be destroyed, will be banished from God's universe. Such is something of their expectation. And supreme happiness must flow from such a state.

Dr. James Reid, the British preacher and author, tells the story of a Christian doctor who on one occasion was visiting a patient who was dying and knew full well his condition. The patient asked the doctor if he could tell him anything about the life that lies beyond death. The doctor was not expecting such a question, and as he paused to consider it before giving his patient an answer, he heard a scratching at the door of the room where they were. That sound gave the doctor a clue. "The noise which you heard," he said, "was made by my little dog. He followed me into the house and is trying to get into the room. He has no idea what he will find here, for he has never been in this room. But he knows that I am here, and that is enough for him."

Dr. Reid says the lesson is obvious. Probably the Christian is as little able to comprehend what awaits him in the many mansions as the dog was to understand what was in the unknown room. But it was enough for him that his master, one whom he loved and trusted, was there. Thus it is with the Christian, and he can say,

> My knowledge of that life is small.
> The eye of faith is dim.
> But 'tis enough that He knows all
> And I shall be with Him.

CHAPTER V

WHAT IS THE RESURRECTION?

ANOTHER EXTREMELY INTERESTING and important question to be considered is, "What becomes of the body at death?" Does it matter what becomes of it? Is it not good riddance for the soul, that it may be free to soar to heights which it was not possible to attain while bound to the body? In a word, did God give man a body only for this life, or, with an intermission, to be his forever?

As with all other great issues of life, there are conflicting opinions as to what the answer to this question is. There are those who claim there is no resurrection of the body. The Lord met with representatives of this group of thought in His day. The Sadducees believed there was to be none, and they sought to entrap Him with all kinds of catch questions concerning the resurrection. These same Sadducees were the bitter opponents of the apostles in the days of the Early Church. They harassed Paul in his work. They live today. It is openly declared, for example, by some professed followers of Christ, that the doctrine of the bodily resurrection is unimportant. The vital thing is the value of the idea, and not the fact of the resurrection. But how can there be value apart from the fact? If it were not a fact, where is the value? Abandon the fact and of necessity the value of the fact will disappear. As another has said, "When the great rock foundations of our faith are reckoned of no account, the values that have accrued may seem to abide, but they will inevitably, even if slowly, lose their transforming power."

The moment one begins to investigate the theories which deny the resurrection of the body, he discovers that there is no general agreement among the opponents of the doctrine. There are those, for example, who deny there is such a thing as a body to rise. That is one extreme. There is a second group who claim that if there is to be any body to be united with the soul in the other life, it must come from Heaven, differing entirely from the earthly body, and bearing no relation to it. It is an entirely new creation, and from materials which never had the least relation to the present body. It is purely a spiritual body. Then there is a third group who claim that the soul will weave about itself a material covering that has nothing in common with a body of any sort. It is not a body at all, but a mere covering for the soul as the garment covers the body in this life.

The scriptural view of the matter is that there is a resurrection of the body of every person, believer and unbeliever. And this is the teaching of the Scripture not by inference only, but is the positive, direct declaration of the whole Word of God. Indeed, if there is one thing which the Scripture emphasizes it is the resurrection. The resurrection of the body is the distinctive teaching of Christianity. The religions of the world, while teaching there is some sort of future existence for man, give no assurance of the resurrection of the human body and its reunion with the soul and spirit to the full restoration of the human being.

The resurrection of the Lord was not a minor detail in the preaching of the apostles, but the most important fact which they had to present. It was the heart of the preaching of Peter on the day of Pentecost (Acts 2:25-36). Paul declared, "And if Christ be not raised, your faith is vain; ye are yet in your sins" (I Cor. 15:17). Moreover, the resurrection of the bodies of believers is conditioned on the resurrection of Christ. His resurrection is the divine assurance that the bodies of all men will be raised from the dead. The resurrection of Christ is described as "the first-fruits" of the great process of resurrection. The reference is to an Old Testament record of a remarkable ceremony which was known as the "wave-offering" and observed statedly by the Israelites. A portion of that record is found in Leviticus 23:9-11: "And the Lord spake unto Moses, saying, Speak unto the children of Israel, and say unto them, When ye be come into the land which I give unto you, and shall reap the harvest thereof, then ye shall bring a sheaf of the firstfruits of your harvest unto the priest: and he shall wave the sheaf before the Lord, to be accepted for you: on the morrow after the sabbath the priest shall wave it." God established this custom among the people and they were careful to observe it. As the time of the harvest approached, they began to walk through their fields of standing grain, plucking here and there a handful of wheat heads, and binding them into a sheaf. This was called the sheaf of the first-fruits. It was taken to the priest who waved it before the Lord as an offering. This was done before the harvest was gathered, and before they themselves had eaten of the harvest.

It should be noted, also, the day of the week on which

the ceremony took place; for there was a time appointed for its observance as definite as was the appointment of the feast itself. The one was just as vital as the other. The priest was to wave this sheaf before the Lord on *the morrow after the Sabbath,* or on the first day of the week; for it was prophetical of the resurrection of Christ from the dead on the first day of the week, and of His becoming "the first-fruits" of them that slept. The sheaf of the first-fruits was a sample of the entire crop to be harvested, and the bringing in of one sheaf was a token that a harvest of similar sheaves would follow. So with the resurrection of Christ. The fact that He was raised from the dead gives assurance that the bodies of all men are to be raised from their graves. The Lord taught His followers to believe this as an assured fact; for He said, "Marvel not at this: for the hour is coming, in the which all that are in the graves shall hear his voice, and shall come forth; they that have done good, unto the resurrection of life; and they that have done evil, unto the resurrection of damnation" (John 5:28, 29). That means, if it means anything, that the body of every child of Adam will some day be raised from its grave.

The redemption of the bodies of believers, moreover, will somehow have direct bearing on the rest and peace of the whole creation. The Scripture teaches that as the whole creation felt the deadly effect of man's sin, so it is to experience the beneficial result of his redemption. "For we know that the whole creation groaneth and travaileth in pain together until now. And not only they, but ourselves also, which have the firstfruits of the Spirit, even we ourselves groan within ourselves, waiting for the adoption, to wit, the redemption of our body" (Rom. 8:22, 23).

Dr. James H. Brooks, the noted preacher and Bible teacher of a generation ago, said, "From the day of the fall to the present hour, creation has been groaning, as if in solemn protest against the sin that wronged and ruined it, if there were only an ear to hear and an eye to see what havoc that sin has made in the once fair domain of earth, and sky, and sea. Musicians say that every note of nature is in the minor key. The sighing of the wind, the dashing of the waves upon the shore, the lowing of the cattle, the song of the birds, all are so pitched that they utter a constant complaint of the injustice they have suffered at the heart of proud and disobedient man."

The peace and well-being of the creature world, therefore, are dependent upon the fact of the resurrection of the body. Since that is the case, is it reasonable to suppose that God will leave humanity and the physical earth in this despairing and hopeless condition forever? If He did, it would indicate that He was defeated in His whole plan for mankind and the world which He created, and which He pronounced good. The last word then would belong to Satan. Death would be the victor, and not God. But this will never happen; for a glorious future is in store, not only for man, but also for the earth.

"The wolf also shall dwell with the lamb, and the leopard shall lie down with the kid; and the calf and the young lion and the fatling together; and a little child shall lead them. And the cow and the bear shall feed; their young ones shall lie down together; and the lion shall eat straw like the ox. And the sucking child shall play on the hole of the asp, and the weaned child shall put his hand on the cockatrice' den. They shall not hurt nor destroy in all my holy mountain: for the earth shall be full of the knowledge of the Lord, as the waters cover the sea" (Isa. 11:6-9). That is not an empty, meaningless promise. It will be fulfilled when He who laid down His life for man's redemption, and bore the thorns, the emblem of the curse, upon His holy brow, comes again, and the bodies of the dead in Him are raised in glory, never again to know sin or taste death.

The Scripture likewise teaches that death is related to Satan, and all his works must be destroyed. "For this purpose the Son of God was manifested, that he might destroy the works of the devil" (I John 3:8). Christ voluntarily died for the sins of His people, entering into the experience of death "that through death he might destroy him that had power of death, that is, the devil" (Heb. 2:14). Thus the problem of the future state becomes simply a question as to whether Christ can accomplish what He set out to do.

At present the Devil has the power of death over the bodies of men, and he has been exercising that power since the days of Adam. But he will not always have it. The Lord will gain the victory. But He will not gain that victory until these corruptible bodies are raised from the dead, and the devil and his emissaries are shut up forever in the lake of fire that is never quenched, reserved forever for them. It means that not a fragment of the purchase of Calvary will be left in the power of the grave. But the undoing of the works of the Devil, which he has wrought in human bodies, will be the last act of the blessed Lord in His redemptive work in behalf of the believer. "The last enemy to be destroyed is death," and that destruction cannot be until "this corruptible shall have put on incorruption, and this mortal shall have put on immortality"; and the moment this is done, and done it shall be, the saying, "Death is swallowed up in victory," shall be gloriously fulfilled.

It may be asked, "Why are we so sure of this?" What are the reasons for believing so positively in the resurrection of the body?

First, *God has signally honored the body.* The Scripture nowhere speaks disparagingly of the worth and dignity of the human body. Christianity honors the body. God has been pleased to make it "the temple of the Holy Ghost" on earth during this age. The body of every believer is indwelt by the Holy Spirit. If God condescends to dwell in the body in its present frail and humiliated condition, how He must value it!

God has not only thus honored the body, but also the body has been supremely honored by the incarnation of the Son of God. He took unto Himself a true body as well as a reasonable soul, and thus became one with man in order that He might redeem him completely, both body and soul. It was with this fact in view the apostle wrote, "Let this mind be in you, which was also in Christ Jesus: who, being in the form of God, thought it not robbery to be equal with God: but made himself of no reputation, and took upon him the form of a servant, and was made in the likeness of men: and being found in fashion as a man, he humbled himself, and became obedient unto death, even the death of the cross. Wherefore God also hath highly exalted him, and given him a name which is above every name: that at the name of Jesus every knee should bow, of things in heaven, and things in earth, and things under the earth; and that every tongue should confess that Jesus Christ is Lord, to the glory of God the Father" (Phil. 2:5-11). Man was originally created in the image of God, but through sin he lost in a measure that image; God gave His only begotten Son to be made in the fashion of man, that man might be restored to that lost estate. And the human body was the instrument of this accomplishment. "The hope of the believer," as it has often been said, "is not deliverance from the body, but redemption of the body." And this redemption appears in God's refashioning it into the likeness of the body of Christ's glory.

A second reason for believing in the resurrection of the body is that *man cannot be a perfect being apart from the body*. Man will be perfect in Heaven. He will be in a perfect place in a perfect condition. That means, if it means anything, that his body, which he left behind him for a little while, will be restored to him. It is for this completion the apostle expresses a longing when he wrote, "For we that are in this tabernacle do groan, being burdened: not for that we would be unclothed, but clothed upon, that mortality might be swallowed up of life" (II Cor. 5:4). It was not the present condition of the departed saints, however happy, which the apostle held before himself, and before those to whom he wrote, as the goal of glorious anticipation, but something even greater which was to follow. When the natural body is raised a spiritual body, the clothed condition is to succeed the unclothed. And is that not how one feels about it? Despite all the blessings and privileges of this present life, the believer groans for a more perfect deliverance from "the bondage of corruption," and the one and only thing that will bring this deliverance is the redemption of the body. The body is a distinct and fundamental part of one's being. Man cannot be made perfect without it. His redemption cannot be fully accomplished apart from it. Hence the crowning act of redemption will be the deliverance of the body from the bondage of corruption in which it is now imprisoned.

A third reason why Christians believe in the resurrection of the body and its continuance in life, is found in the significance of the term *resurrection*. The Scripture employs the word "resurrection" with considerable frequency, and always uses it in the sense of bringing back to activity a body once dead. Take this one passage, I Corinthians 15. This chapter is the full discussion of God's revelation concerning the resurrection of the body, and in it special emphasis is laid on the fact that what is placed in the grave is what comes out of the grave. The soul does not go down to the grave; it departs immediately to be with Christ which is far better than living here. But that is not the complete state. Happy and glorious as that state must be, a sense of incompleteness is felt, and will continue to be felt until the soul and body are reunited. As only the body is put into the grave, nothing but the body belonging to man can come out of it.

But there is more in the word "resurrection" than merely bringing back to activity. It signifies, also, that the body will be restored to the highest possible degree of perfection. Sin wrought havoc with the body, yet not only will it be restored to its highest degree of perfection, but will be refashioned after a new pattern. "And we know that all things work together for good to them that love God, to them who are the called according to his purpose. For whom he did foreknow, he also did predestinate"—to what?—"to be conformed to the image of his Son, that he might be the firstborn among many brethren" (Rom. 8:28, 29).

God did not allow the Devil to get possession of the body of Moses, though Satan contended with all his might for it (Jude 9). Why? Because Moses had use for that body. If God did not allow the body of Moses to fall into the hands of the Devil, neither will He allow the Devil, or any other power, to keep the body of the believer from being resurrected and united with his soul at the coming of the Lord.

In the fourth place, the Christian believes in the resurrection of the body and its continuance in life forever because that seems to be *the only logical and sensible conclusion of human life here,* in view of God's marvelous estimate of the worth of man and the cost He paid for his redemption. Man is God's creature. He was not only created by God, but created in the image and after the likeness of God. God is eternal. Man is, as far as is known, the last, the highest, the richest, the ripest fruit of God's cosmic effort. Man is the most precious thing God has on earth. All this seems evident in the fact that when man defaced the image of God in him, God, at the cost of the incarnation of His only begotten Son, in the likeness of man, and by His death on the cross, made it possible in the course of time for man to be restored to his former state and condition. The very facts of how God created the body of man and what He has done to rescue man from his fallen state are convincing evidences that God is going to do what He has declared to be His intention: raise up the body at the last day.

In the fifth place, the resurrection is believed to be true *because of the term used in the New Testament to describe bodily death.* The term is "sleep." By the atoning work of Christ in man's behalf, the term is no longer "death" but merely "sleep." Read the New Testament carefully to note the number of times sleep is used to describe death: "She is not dead, but *sleepeth*"; "our friend Lazarus *sleepeth*"; David after he had served his own generation by the will of God, fell on *"sleep"*; Stephen *"fell asleep"*; "we shall not all *sleep*"; "them also which *sleep* in Jesus"; these are only a few of the many examples of the use of the word one will find. Hence, the early Christians called the burial grounds "cemeteries," that is, "sleeping places," where they laid the bodies of their dearest friends to take their quiet rest. The expression is sweetly significant.

Sleep is transitory. It implies a reawakening. The Bible calls bodily death a "sleep" for the reason that the death state is not eternal, but only temporary, from which there is presently to come a rising up again. This is not sleep which has no awakening to follow. It is said that at three o'clock one morning, Dr. A. T. Pierson received a telegram, asking him to preach the sermon at the funeral of Dr. A. J. Gordon. Unable to sleep, he spent the rest of the night searching his Greek Testament for what it said about death. He made an important discovery. To the great throng gathered for the occasion he told of his surprise to find that after the resurrection the apostles never used the word "death" to express the close of a Christian's earthly life; but referred to the passing of a Christian as "at home with the Lord . . . to depart and be with Christ . . . to sleep in Jesus . . . fallen asleep . . . loosing the moorings . . . forever with the Lord," and similar terms.

It cannot be insisted upon too strongly that it is the same body that is put into the grave that is raised. There has been and still is a good deal of teaching about a "spiritual resurrection." Whatever scriptural basis there may appear to be for this theory centers in I Corinthians 15:44: "It is raised a spiritual body." The Greek word *soma,* translated "body" in this passage, is used ten times in this chapter, and in each instance evidently refers to the actual material body. And what is true of the use of the word in this chapter applies to its use throughout the New Testament (Matt. 6:25; Mark 5:29; Luke 12:4; John 19:40). Why then try to make it mean something else when its import is clearly evident?

Such scriptures as Romans 8:11, which states that the mortal bodies will be quickened; Romans 8:23, which puts before the Christian the hope of the redemption of the body; and Matthew 27:52, which distinctly states that the *bodies* of the saints arose—all are utterly meaningless unless understood literally. In His prophetic Olivet discourse the Lord Jesus said to His disciples that they would be betrayed by false brethren and friends, "and some of you shall they cause to be put to death." And then, almost immediately He makes a strange statement: "But there shall not an hair of your head perish" (Luke 21:16, 18). What does this mean? Either it is highly figurative, a hyperbole of the most extreme sort, or else it is a quiet, literal statement of fact. And it is always safest in interpreting Scripture to take the statement literally unless the context demands that it be understood figuratively—which is not so here. Further proof of this is God's numbering the hairs of the head—not an idle amusement of Deity. In view of the other revelations of Scripture plainly declaring the resurrection of the bodies of believers, one may well believe the Lord was promising literal bodily resurrection to those who should lay down their lives under persecution because of their faithful testimony to Him. To include the hairs of the head in the resurrection victory may seem staggeringly miraculous, of course—but what is too hard for God?

A final reason for the Christian belief is that *Christ must reign*. That is an assured fact. There are many changes to transpire in the affairs of earth, but what these are to be, is unknown to man. But the last act of time is known, for it has been revealed. It will not be man's act, but God's act. It is written, "Then cometh the end, when he shall have delivered up the kingdom to God, even the Father; when he shall have put down all rule and all authority and power. For he must reign, till he hath put all enemies under his feet. The last enemy that shall be destroyed is death. . . . And when all things shall be subdued unto him, then shall the Son also himself be subject unto him that put all things under him, that God may be all in all" (I Cor. 15:24-28). Hence there is a divine necessity for the resurrection of the body, and that necessity lies in the fact that "He must reign." Thank God, He shall reign, and His saints with Him in their resurrected bodies, "fashioned like unto his glorious body, according to the working whereby he is able even to subdue all things unto himself" (Phil. 3:21). The resurrection of the body is sure, "for he must reign."

Chapter VI

WHAT IS THE NATURE OF THE RESURRECTION BODY?

The resurrection not only is distinctly taught in Scripture but is one of the cardinal doctrines. Take this doctrine out of the Bible and the foundation stone of Christian faith is removed. Paul declares the resurrection to be the sum and substance of the gospel which he faithfully preached and for which he gladly died.

Reassuring as the doctrine of the resurrection is, however, it does not altogether satisfy the inquiring soul seeking light on the life beyond. He wants to know more than the mere fact of the resurrection of the body. He wants to know what kind of body it will be. God has been pleased to provide ample information on this subject to satisfy the desire of any reasonable person. While He has not revealed all that one might wish to know, He has given the great central facts; and the details are matters for faith. Since God always keeps His word, He can be trusted to give to each individual not only his own body, but with such changes as to make it best suited to the requirements of its new surroundings.

Among the first questions usually asked, when the subject of the resurrection is under consideration, are these: "How are the dead raised up?" and "With what bodies do they come?" Sometimes these are questions of unbelief or doubt; sometimes of mere curiosity; but most generally they are prompted by perplexity or anxious fear. For example, when the bodies of loved ones and friends are laid away in extreme weakness, or maimed by accident, one wants to know what kind of bodies they are to have in the resurrection. Will the bodies of these friends be raised in their weakened and maimed condition, or will they be restored to the freshness of youth and the vigor of full manhood which they once knew? Or will they be given entirely different bodies? These are questions of vital concern and are worthy of serious consideration.

The only source of information on all questions having to do with the future life is the Word of God. What answer does it give to these questions pressing so heavily upon the hearts and minds of sorrowing ones throughout the world?

The Bible declares there is to be a marvelous difference between what the believer is here and what he shall be in Heaven. It could not be otherwise, for the life and environment of Heaven must be entirely different from that of a fallen race in a lost and sinful world. But with all the difference, each believer will still be himself and not another person. He will carry with him into Heaven, and retain forever, his personal identity. And this identity of person applies as truly to the body as to any other part of his being. He will most certainly not be less a person in his resurrection body than he was in his earthly one. Whatever changes are made in the body, it will still be the body he had in this life, the one in which he toiled and suffered, loved and rejoiced, and at last died.

Now it might be less difficult for some to believe that at the resurrection, instead of the present body, they will receive an entirely new one, bearing no relation whatever to the present, mortal body. And there are those who argue in favor of such a theory. They claim that it would be far easier and much more logical for God to create an entirely new body from fresh dust of the earth, or of some other appropriate material found elsewhere in His universe, than to search out the scattered dust of dead bodies and refashion them, and give them again to the myriad hosts of disembodied spirits who once possessed them. Now that view may sound plausible to some, but it will not require much thought to discover how unsound it is. If this conception were true, one could hardly speak of a resurrection; for if that which has become dust does not rise, something new must take its place, and that is not resurrection. In that event there would be no conceivable reason why the Scripture should speak of the body coming forth from the grave. For it is not the soul, and spirit that are interred, but the body, and only the body. Unless the body is raised there would be no resurrection, and the Scripture would create a grave misapprehension concerning the whole matter. And surely no one is willing to go that far. But the Scripture leaves no room for doubt on this matter. It teaches directly and positively, *not* by inference *only*, that the spirit will necessarily receive its own body again.

The believer is taught that Christ is the first fruits of them that sleep. That is to say, His resurrection is a sample and an assurance of the resurrection of the body. What kind of body did He have after His resurrection? Was it the same as the one which was put into Joseph's new tomb, and that tomb sealed by the authority of the Roman government? What were the Roman government and the Jews—particularly the Jews—so concerned about? Was it not His body? The one thing above all others which they would keep undisturbed was the burial place of the Lord. Every bit of power which could be exerted by the Jews, with the assistance of the Roman government, was exercised to prevent His body coming out of the grave. But they were not able to do so. After three days He appeared in His body to His disciples. What happened? They did not recognize Him immediately. Indeed, they thought He was an apparition, a spirit. But He began at once to convince them of His identity—to prove He was the same person whom they had seen die on the cross. How does He convince them? By proving to them His body was the same body. He says to them: "Behold my hands and my feet, that it is I myself: handle me, and see; for a spirit hath not flesh and bones, as ye see me have" (Luke 24:39). To Thomas He said: "Reach hither thy finger, and behold my hands; and reach hither thy hand, and thrust it into my side: and be not faithless, but believing" (John 20:27). He based His appeal for recognition on the fact that He was there in the same body. And when Thomas saw the body, the wounds, the scars, he cried, "My Lord and my God." The Lord went even further. He took a piece of fish and some honey and ate it before their eyes. Why? Because He needed food? No; but to convince them beyond the shadow of doubt that He was the same Lord, appearing to them in the identical body which they had seen mangled on the cross. Now since Christ has risen from the dead and "become the first fruits of them that slept," there is not the slightest doubt but that the believer's body will be raised and vivified with new and eternal life.

Will there be any difference between the present body and the resurrection body? Most definitely there will be. Identity does not require that the body be raised from the grave exactly as it was laid in it. If it did, that would not be a very pleasant anticipation for many. A person wants this present body, but he does not necessarily want it as it is. For example, one often meets the deformed, the crippled, the invalid, the blind, the deaf, and those with other imperfections.

But these are *defects* that do not belong to the body as such. The body has been terribly maimed by sin and by disease, which is the result of sin. God did not fashion the body in that way. The human body was perfect when it came from the hand of God. There was not a single defect in all the complex mechanism of the human body when God created it. All these imperfections and defects and weaknesses and the like are the result of the catastrophe which overtook man in the Fall. It is a part of the wages of sin.

But God was not pleased to leave man in his fallen state. He provided salvation for him. And by the blood of the crucified Redeemer, man was rescued from that terrible state and brought back into the family of God. Did He redeem only a portion of man? No; His redemption reaches to man's last and least interest. Is it conceivable that God, who endowed man with such a marvelous body, would allow it to be wrecked forever? It is not possible that He would. We can be sure that when the body is raised all these defects and imperfections will be entirely and forever removed. It will again be a perfect body. Perfection excludes all that is weak, and sick, and immature. Imperfection does not harmonize with the new Heaven and the new earth. It will be the same body, wearing again the nobility of the image and likeness of God.

It is likewise evident from the Scripture that while the two bodies are identical in essence they are different in qualities. Someone has illustrated this change in qualities in this way. Water, snow, ice, and vapor are in essence the same. Within the range of a few degrees of temperature the one changes into the other, and even though it seems to have become something else, it remains water. You can easily change the snow or ice back to water again; and you have only to condense the vapor and you have drops of water. In each case you have similarity of essence, but the qualities are different. You sink in water, but your body is supported by ice. The snowflakes descend, and the vapor rises, yet in essence they are the same. The only difference lies in the qualities of each as the water assumes a new form.

Now after the same fashion a change will take place in the body. It will be changed from the common to the noble, from the humiliated to the glorified, yet in essence it is the same body.

As to the fashion of the resurrected body, the Bible teaches that it will be made conformable to the body of glory of Christ Himself. "For our conversation [citizenship] is in heaven; from whence also we look for the Saviour, the Lord Jesus Christ: who shall change our vile body [body of humiliation], that it may be fashioned like unto his glorious body [body of glory], according to the working whereby he is able even to subdue all things unto himself" (Phil. 3:20, 21). What is known of Christ's body of glory? What is its fashion? What was it like when His disciples saw Him go up in His body into the clouds out of their sight? Are any of its characteristics known? Yes, a number of them have been made quite evident.

First, *it was visible.* It was something they could see and touch and handle. In other words, it had substance. He was visible to His disciples at intervals for forty days in His resurrection body before His ascension. They had ample time and opportunity to observe His body. It was in the body that He made Himself visible to them. He appeared to individuals, to groups of individuals, and on one occasion to a company of more than five hundred. And He was visible after His ascension. Stephen, as he was being stoned to death, saw Him. Looking steadfastly into Heaven he exclaimed: "Behold, I see the heavens opened, and the Son of man standing on the right hand of God" (Acts 7:56). Paul saw Him on more than one occasion. John saw Him, and so glorious was His appearance that he fell at His feet as dead. Since the bodies of believers are to be fashioned like unto His body of glory, certainly visibility will be one of their qualities.

Second, *it was a real body,* and not some apparition, as the disciples at first thought. He appeared not as a disembodied spirit. The one thing He sought to dislodge from the minds of His disciples was that He was now only a spirit. He said to them: "A spirit hath not flesh and bones as ye see me have." He even allowed them to handle Him to convince them that He was with them in a real, true body. And years later when John writes an epistle, the object of which was to lead the believer into the full assurance of faith (I John 5:13), he began it by declaring: "That which was from the beginning, which we have heard, which we have seen with our eyes, which we have looked upon, and our hands have handled, of the Word of life" (I John 1:1), which evidently refers to the time when the disciples were allowed to touch His risen body.

He ate food before them. Does that imply that the resurrection body must be nourished with food and drink? Not at all, for Jesus did not eat to nourish His body, but simply to prove that it was a real body. And when He appeared to His disciples that morning at the Sea of Tiberius, they recognized Him while they were some distance at sea. He is said to have eaten again, which indicates that He wanted His disciples to know that His body was a true one. Since the body of the believer is to be like Christ's present body, it, too, will be just as real as is His body.

Third, *it was a glorified body*. John, the beloved disciple, was permitted to see in vision something of the glory of Christ's present body. One day while he was on the isle that is called Patmos, for the Word of God, and for the testimony of Jesus Christ, he saw the Son of Man in the midst of the seven candlesticks—the risen Christ—clothed with a garment down to the foot, and girt about the paps with a golden girdle. His head and His hairs were white like wool, as white as snow; and His eyes were as a flame of fire; and His feet like unto fine brass, and His voice as the sound of many waters, and He had in His right hand seven stars, and His countenance was as the sun shines in his strength (Rev. 1:12-16). Whatever else may be involved in this description, it most assuredly means to convey the fact that Christ's risen body was a real, visible, glorious one.

Paul describes His resurrection body as "the body of glory," and insists that the bodies of believers will be conformable to it. There are four great contrasts given in I Corinthians 15:42-44, between the natural body which is subject to death, and the spiritual or resurrection body which will never die. In these four contrasts Paul does not refer solely to the condition of the body at the moment of death or to when it is buried, but gives a picture of the whole bodily existence on this side of the grave. He does this in order that he may compare it with existence, not only at the moment of the resurrection, but throughout eternity. Note the contrasts:

The first contrast is that of *corruption and incorruption*. The present body is subject to decay and corruption. That point need not be argued. Disease is always at work. But how different will be the resurrection body! It will never grow tired, the head will never ache, and the heart will never faint.

The second contrast is that of *dishonor and glory*. It is not so easy to think of the body as presently constituted as one of dishonor. One is rather inclined to exalt the body by praising its grandeur and glory. It is difficult to believe that the present body has the stamp of dishonor upon it, because one has never seen a body anywhere else but here, or under any other condition except as seen here. Nothing is known of the appearance of the body before sin struck it such a fatal blow. If one could compare the present body with the body of man as it was originally created, what a striking contrast would be apparent! No doubt one would exclaim, "How are the mighty fallen!" It would be easy then to admit that much of the honor and glory with which the body was originally invested has departed, and that it is at best but a shell of its former self. Its glory now is but the remains of the original glory. And there is not much reason to be proud and boastful of a body that is so often full of aches and pains; that has to be patched up continually to keep it living; that grows old and feeble in a few brief years, and then finally falls into utter decay.

But this will not be true of the body of glory which will be fashioned from this present one. Then the believer will have a perfect body shining in the luster of eternal life. An incident in the life of Moses gives a dim picture of what it will be. It is related that when he came down from the mountain after his interview with God, his face shone with such glory that he had to cover it before the people. And is there not also a suggestion of the glory of the resurrection body in the transfiguration of the body of the Lord on the holy mount? There Peter, James, and John beheld His body as it shone with glorious luster. As the believer's body is to be like His body of glory, is there not here at least some semblance of what the resurrection body will be like?

The third contrast is that of *weakness and power.* Man may boast of his strength, but he knows well that he is not any too strong. Physically, man is weak. He cannot endure much. Many tasks are undone simply because he has not the strength to finish them. He would do more if only he had the power.

And then, as the years go by, whatever little strength he possesses gradually diminishes until it is all gone and he ceases activity altogether. He soon becomes not only too frail for the ordinary tasks of life, but even to take care of himself. That is one of the things which people most dread about growing old. They say "we do not want to be a bother to anyone." They do not wish to be a care to anyone, even to their dearest ones.

But of the new body it never can be said there is not sufficient power, for it will be equal to all the requirements of the eternal life. It will never grow weary; never become exhausted; never have to fail because of lack of strength. The power that wrought in the Lord's body when He was raised from the dead is the power that is at work in the Christian's life. This power not only raised Him from the dead, but exalted Him to the right hand of God, "Far above all principality, and power, and might, and dominion, and every name that is named, not only in this world, but also in that which is to come: and hath put all things under his feet, and gave him to be the head over all things to the church, which is his body, the fulness of him that filleth all in all" (Eph. 1:21-23). That same power will work in the believer's body, not only to raise it from the dead, but to bring it into the likeness of His own glorious body, and to keep it in all its perfection throughout the ages of eternity.

There is one other contrast. This one is between *the natural and the spiritual body.* That means that the Spirit of God, who makes these bodies His temple while they are here on earth, will have full possession of the new body, and that it will be wholly adapted to the new heavenly environment, even in a far greater sense than this present body is adapted to its present environment.

And let it be remembered that, despite all the changes to be wrought in these bodies, *individuality will not be lost*. Whatever change may be undergone, this much is clear: each person will receive a body fitted to his personality, and through which he may fitly express himself. The individuality that characterizes people now, and differentiates them from each other, will also be theirs in the state of glory.

The inevitable conclusion then is the believer will not only live, but be his own true self in the life beyond. That is not true of him now. He cannot be his best self here. There is too much wrong with him. But before he enters upon that eternal existence in the resurrection body, all grossness, all imperfection, all immaturity will have been completely and forever removed in order that there will be nothing to hinder him. Personal identity will be retained forever, and God will give to each his own body. Surely it is enough to satisfy anyone to know that his body will be like Christ's own glorious body throughout eternity!

CHAPTER VII

WHAT IS THE BELIEVER'S JUDGMENT?

AFTER THE RESURRECTION the next great event to transpire, as far as the Scripture indicates, is the judgment. With the possible exception of death, no future event so fills the heart of the average person with awe and dread as the thought of the judgment. It is a subject about which little is heard and less is known. And yet it is a matter which should be the concern of everyone, for no one is to escape judgment. "It is appointed unto men once to die, but after this the judgment." In speaking to the Athenians on Mars' hill, Paul declared that God "now commandeth all men everywhere to repent. Because he hath appointed a day, in the which he will judge the world in righteousness by that man whom he hath ordained; whereof he hath given assurance unto all men, in that he hath raised him from the dead" (Acts 17:30, 31). The day for the judgment has been appointed. The judge has been ordained for the occasion. It is sure, for it belongs to the unchangeable appointments of God.

There are two general groups of people who are to be the subjects of judgment. These groups are composed of believers and unbelievers. The judgment now under consideration is limited to that of the believer. The purpose of the appearing in judgment of the believer is quite different from that of the unbeliever. In the case of the unbeliever, the judgment has to do with his sins and future punishment; whereas the believer's works are judged and his reward bestowed.

The place of the believer's judgment is "the judgment seat of Christ." In writing to bereaved Christians at Corinth, Paul says: "For we must all appear before the judgment seat of Christ; that everyone may receive the things done in his body, according to that he hath done, whether it be good or bad" (II Cor. 5:10). The question here is not the believer's sins, but his works. The sins of the believer have been atoned for by his Judge, Jesus Christ, and are remembered no more forever (Heb. 10:17). But every "work" must come unto judgment (Matt. 12:36; Eph. 6:8; Col. 3:24, 25).

The result of the believer's judgment is reward or loss of reward "but he himself shall be saved" (I Cor. 3:11-15). If his works are "good" he shall receive due reward and shall not be ashamed; but if on the other hand his works are "bad," they will be destroyed and he will have no reward.

But someone says, is not every judgment throne to be considered as the judgment seat of Christ? Does He not declare that "the Father judgeth no man, but hath committed all judgment unto the Son" (John 5:22)? This is true. Christ as the resurrected Man has been ordained by God as the Judge of all (Acts 17:31). Both the living and the dead are to give an account to Him, whether saved or unsaved (I Peter 4:5; Acts 10:42). But the point is, the believer, unlike the unbeliever, will never be subject to condemnatory judgment. For him all such judgment is past (John 5:24). Yet, while this is blessedly true, it is a solemn fact, nevertheless, that all must stand before the judgment seat of Christ to receive the things done in the body whether they be good or bad. So impressed was Paul at the thought of the judgment that he declares that his constant ambition is so to deport himself, and so to be diligent in service, that he shall be able to give an account of his stewardship with joy at that great tribunal.

The Lord Jesus Christ, who is to be the Judge of the believer, gives a vivid picture of this judgment in one of His matchless parables. He tells of the man who, before making a journey into a far country, called his own servants and delivered unto them his goods, giving to one five talents, to another two, and to another one: "to every man according to his several ability," that they might use them to his advantage during his absence. The servant that had received five talents "made of them other five talents." And the one that received two also gained other two. "But he that had received one went and digged in the earth, and hid his lord's money." What happened when the lord of those servants returned? With those who had received the five talents and the two talents, he was pleased and rewarded them according to their works. But the one who failed to make use of the one talent entrusted to him not only received no reward but was dispossessed of what he had.

From the Scripture it is evident that at "the judgment seat of Christ" only the believer will be there. It would seem that the little pronoun *we* in II Corinthians 5 definitely decides this question. The chapter is not a very long one, but in it the word "we" occurs twenty-six times, and in every instance it refers only to believers. That only believers are meant is even more clearly seen when the connections of the pronoun are noted. "*We* know"; "*we* have"; "*we* groan"; "*we* walk"; "*we* are confident"; "*we* labor"; "*we* may be accepted." When the plural pronoun *we* is used in any of the epistles, believers, and only believers, are meant. Dr. James Denney says, "It is Christians who only are in view here." Indeed, as is well-known, the entire epistle is addressed to saints, and not to sinners (II Cor. 1:1). Therefore, the inference is clear that only believers in the character of servants, will be there.

What is the purpose of the judgment at which the believer is to appear? The common opinion is to regard it as a "trial" to decide whether men are saved or eternally lost. And because of this view of the purpose of the judgment they live in a state of uncertainty all their lives. Robert Ingersoll, the well-known agnostic of a generation ago, in one of his poems says:

> Is there beyond the silent night an endless day?
> Is death a door that leads to light? We cannot say.
> The tongueless secret locked in fate,
> We do not know, we hope and wait.

That is the language of agnosticism, and yet there are multitudes of nominal Christians using similar language, when faced with the solemn and searching question relative to eternity. "We do not know, we hope and wait." But the Christian who knows Jesus Christ in the forgiveness of sin, faces no "tongueless secret locked in fate," concerning his place in eternity. For just as surely as Jesus Christ shed His blood to put away sin, God has given us the Bible to put away all doubts equally as far as Jesus' blood has put away forgiven sin. Listen to the language of the instructed believer, as it is heard down the ages. "I *know* that my redeemer liveth, and that he shall stand at the latter day upon the earth: and though after my skin worms destroy this body, yet in my flesh shall I see God" (Job 19:25, 26). "We *know* that if our earthly house of this tabernacle were dissolved, we *have* a building of God, an house not made with hands, eternal in the heavens" (II Cor. 5:1). "I *know* whom I have believed, and am persuaded that he is able to keep that which I have committed unto him against that day" (II Tim. 1:12). No; believers do not have to "hope and wait" until the judgment seat of Christ to know whether they are saved or unsaved. They rest their future on the finished work of Christ, and on the assurance of His unfailing promise they face the future without a fear.

The judgment is not to be a trial to decide the fate either of the saved or of the unsaved. Men need not live in suspense until the day of judgment to know their eternal state. The Bible speaks plainly and definitely on this subject, and if he will only believe what the Bible says, one need not be in doubt for one moment. This one passage is enough to settle this point: "For God so loved the world, that he gave his only begotten Son, that whosoever believeth in him should not perish, but have everlasting life. For God sent not his Son into the world to condemn the world; but that the world through him might be saved. He that believeth on him is not condemned: but he that believeth not is condemned already, because he hath not believed in the name of the only begotten Son of God" (John 3:16-18). It is unthinkable to suppose that the apostle Paul, who served faithfully, and finally sealed his testimony with his own life, after being now for nearly nineteen hundred years with the Lord, is to appear at the judgment seat of Christ to learn whether his eternal destiny shall be life or death, Heaven or Hell.

As to the purpose of this judgment, Principal Moule says, on Romans 14:10, "We have seen here, as in II Corinthians 5:10, and again, under other imagery, in I Corinthans 3:11-15, a glimpse of that heart-searching prospect for the Christian, his summons hereafter, *as a Christian,* to the tribunal of his Lord. In all the three passages, and now particularly in this, the language is limited by the context, as to its direct purpose, to the Master's *scrutiny of His own servants as such.* The question to be tried and decided (speaking after the manner of men) at His tribunal, in this reference, is not that of glory or perdition; the persons of the examined are accepted; the inquiry is in the *domestic* court of the Palace, so to speak; it regards the reward of the King as to the issue and value of His accepted servants' labor and conduct, as His representatives, in their mortal life. 'The Lord *of those servants* cometh and reckoneth *with them.*' " They shall be saved whatever be the fate of their "works." All this is brought out in I Corinthians 3:11-15.

God's work for the believer places him, as to his standing, on new ground, beyond the judgment for sin, beyond its doom, beyond its death, in a new life in which he can now serve God, and in which he can stand with joy at the judgment seat of Christ. It is a life beyond death and beyond the judgment. All believers have this immunity, whether they realize it or not. The Word of

God has settled all, and it is unbelief to doubt it (John 3:16, 18, 36; 5:24; Rom. 8:1).

Whatever else may be the purpose of this judgment, therefore, it is not to decide whether the believer shall enter Heaven or not. "There is therefore now no condemnation for them who are in Christ Jesus." For them the sin question has been settled, and settled forever. "For he hath made him to be sin for us, who knew no sin; that we might be made the righteousness of God in him" (II Corinthians 5:21). "Who his own self bare our sins in his own body on the tree" (I Peter 2:24). "For Christ also hath once suffered for sins, the just for the unjust" (I Peter 3:18).

All the saved will together enjoy perfect salvation. God does not make the one less in salvation than the other. Half a salvation would even be an incongruity. Those who would be but partly saved would ever have some unfulfilled desire to haunt them. There is, therefore, one salvation, alike for all. It makes no difference whether one has endured the burden and heat of the day because he was called in his youth and has served Him all life long with sorrow and care, or has come to the knowledge of the truth in old age, and has therefore been able to do but little or nothing to express his gratitude to the Saviour for the grace received at the eleventh hour. They all have full and complete salvation—no matter how poor, how rich, how young, how old, how long they have served, or how short.

While the purpose of this judgment is not to decide one's destination, it will decide the *degree of glory* to which the believer will attain in the future. Each will receive a reward according to his works, not a reward in the common, ordinary sense of pay for service, but a reward of grace. God is not unrighteous that He should forget the work and the labor of love that His child wrought in His name while on earth. Each will surely receive a reward of grace—and this reward will be in accordance with his works. A reward for what he has suffered and sacrificed for Christ's sake; for the proper use of talents entrusted to his care; for the love he has shown his enemies; for the help given the poor; for the sick visited in His blessed name—these shall bring their reward.

While the salvation will, therefore, be the same for all the redeemed, the glory of each will not be the same, the difference being determined by the fruits of their lives on earth. Each one will receive such a measure of glory as is fitting for him alone; because it is in harmony with his capacity and ability. Every good deed done develops character, and tends to ennoble personality. No one will receive less glory than he deserves, or more than he can bear.

And no one need fear that envy or jealousy will spring up among the redeemed over their respective rewards. Each one will be perfectly satisfied when he "awakes in His likeness," and receives his reward for the things done on earth in the body. There will be no place for unholy passions and desires in the hearts of those who have "come in the unity of the faith, and of the knowledge of the Son of God, unto a perfect man, unto the measure of the stature of the fullness of Christ" (Eph. 4:13).

Since the reward is now being laid up by believers in Heaven, it behooves them to make the service of Christ their chief business on earth. By diligent service they should seek to lay up for themselves "treasures in heaven, where neither moth nor rust doth corrupt, and where thieves do not break through nor steal" (Matt. 6:19, 20). They can well afford to do this, for both the believer and the treasures are eternally secure.

But what about the sins of the believer? Will these not all be there to face him to his shame and dismay? That they will be is the idea many have, but it is not according to God's Word.

First, the sins committed by the believer *before* he became a Christian will not be there to plague him, because they are all forgiven and forgotten. "And their sins and iniquities will I remember no more" (Heb. 10:17; Rom. 3:5). The fact that the believer's sins are forgiven and forgotten is strikingly illustrated in Hebrews 11. In this chapter is an account of what faith in God did for the Old Testament saints. There is a remarkable thing about this record. Were there no other account of these men and women, one would suppose that they were perfect specimens of believers—that their lives were without flaw. But such is not the case. Some of them were pretty bad sinners at one time in their lives, and none of them ever reached a state of perfection in this life so far as practice is concerned. But in this chapter there is not a word about the failure of a single one of them. Why is this? There must be some good reason for this omission. The reason is stated in the previous chapter; God had said, "And their sins and iniquities will I remember no more" (Heb. 10:17). If He had recorded their sins in the following chapter, it would have shown that He had not forgotten them. Since the sins of the Christian are forgiven and forgotten, therefore, they cannot, and will not, be brought up at the judgment seat of Christ.

Second, the believer's sins committed and confessed *after* he has become a Christian will not be brought up at the judgment seat of Christ. Sins confessed are forgiven. If he does not confess his sins after he becomes a Christian, the Lord deals with him in chastisement (Heb. 12); but "If we confess our sins, he is faithful and just to forgive us our sins, and to cleanse us from all unrighteousness" (I John 1:9).

Hence, the truth taught here is that the sin question, in a penal sense, will never be opened, for that was settled at the cross. Christ died for the sins of believers according to the Scripture; and owing to His atoning death, all sins are put away; they are forgiven forever, never to be brought up again, neither in this world nor in the one to come.

"But," say some, "what of the scars of sin?" Perhaps they cite the illustration of driving a nail into a post and calling attention to the fact that when the nail is pulled out it leaves a scar. In a similar way, they say, though one's sins are forgiven, the scars remain. But those who argue thus forget that "he was wounded for our transgressions, he was bruised for our iniquities" (Isa. 53:5). Christ bears the marks, the scars of sin. The mark is in His hand and the scars are in His wounded side. With this truth before him, the Christian should not allow the past to haunt him; neither should he brood over it. Paul set an example: "Forgetting the things which are behind" (Phil. 3:13). And Paul had much to forget.

Third, at the judgment seat of Christ three things will occur: First, *the Son of God Himself shall be manifested.*

When He came to die for men they did not recognize Him as the Son of God, because He "made himself of no reputation, and took upon him the form of a servant, and was made in the likeness of men: and being found in fashion as a man, he humbled himself, and became obedient unto death, even the death of the cross" (Phil. 2:7, 8). Isaiah, eight hundred years before Christ came, prophesied that when He should appear, He would have "no form nor comeliness" and there would be "no beauty that we should desire him"; that He would be "despised and rejected of men; a man of sorrows, and acquainted with grief" (Isa. 53:2, 3). But all will be changed when He appears again. When Christ was on earth the question was often asked, "Who is he?" He was not then recognized by men as the Son of God, the Saviour of the world; but when He occupies His judgment seat, He shall be seen in the full blaze of glory which He had with the Father before He came to earth.

The second thing to take place at the judgment seat will be *the manifestation of the sons of God in glory.* John says, "It doth not yet appear what we shall be: but we know that, when he shall appear, we shall be like him; for we shall see him as he is" (I John 3:2). At the present time the believer does not rank in the estimation of the world. His is a lowly, humble sort of life. His value to human society is not recognized, just as Lot's life was not valued in Sodom. Yet God said He could do nothing toward destroying that city until Lot and those with him were removed. Today the Christian is "the salt of the earth" and "the light of the world." He does not, however, appear to be particularly indispensable. But at the judgment seat his true worth will be seen. What a revelation that will be when the sons of God are manifested! Then shall every man have his praise of God (I Cor. 4:5; Rev. 7:14; 19:8, 14; 22:4).

The third thing to occur at the judgment seat of Christ will be *the appraisal of the believer's works and the distribution of the rewards.* "Every man's work shall be made manifest: for the day shall declare it, because it shall be revealed by fire; and the fire shall try every man's work of what sort it is" (I Cor. 3:13). Is there anything so calculated to stir the Christian to greater activity than this fire test of all his works? How careful, then, he should be to scrutinize even his best motives, lest he be found performing his service only to be seen of men and to have their praise! He should remember always that no matter how apparently successful he may be in his activities, these will all go for naught unless done in the name and for the sake of Christ Jesus who is to be the final judge of them all. All he may do otherwise, no matter how much it may please men, is only building out of "wood, hay, and stubble," materials which cannot abide the fire.

All should remember, therefore, that Christian service is not just any good deed one may choose to perform, for the child of God has been created in Christ Jesus unto good works, *which God hath before ordained that he should walk in them* (Eph. 2:10). Some think that they can do very much as they please, and receive a full reward. That is building with "wood, hay and stubble." It is only as Christians walk in the work which God has ordained that they receive a reward. This means there is a definite field of service divinely planned for each one, and that "good works" in the Biblical sense can only be in finding and doing that which He has ordained. The works are *good* only as they are done according to "the good and acceptable, and perfect will of God" for each one. These can only be entered into by His direction, which will be realized by all who wholly yield to Him. Such service must be *where He wills,* and the believer should be careful to maintain good works (Titus 2:14; 3:8), according to the divine appointment.

God has graciously promised to recognize all service that is rendered as an expression of love to Him, and is within the gracious plan of life He has for every child of His. There will be rewards, crowns, and prizes. No one can say definitely just what these are, but they most evidently speak of His loving appreciation of service, suffering, and faithfulness to Him. These rewards will be inexpressibly sweet, and will abide for eternity. Then how important it is that the Christian should build with the material of God's truth and according to His will! For as another has said: "The shoddiness of a social gospel, the tinsel of a semireligious and worldly entertainment, the blare and flare of human exhibitions, the whitewash of empty and powerless ethics, the humanitarianism which is based on mere selfism, and the self-inflation of rationalism, and the externalism of dressy ritualism, are materials which will be fuel for the fire of his judgment."

Finally, this judgment will mark the beginning of the "ages to come" in which God will "show the exceeding riches of his grace in his kindness toward us through Christ Jesus" (Eph. 2:7). There will be seen then, in the fully redeemed child of God in glory, something of the measure of God's marvelous grace in His work of redemption. There the believer will be placed on exhibition, as it were, before all sentient creation as the manifestation of what God's grace could do, and did do, in saving, cleansing, and keeping poor, frail man, who had been dead in trespasses and sins. What marvelous manifestations will be unfolded on that day! Christ, in all His glory, will be manifested; the sons of God who trusted in Him, and were not ashamed, will be seen as they are; all the works which they did in His name and for His sake will be visible, and all to the praise and honor of His blessed name. To all who love His appearing, therefore, the judgment seat of Christ has no terror; for it will be their "crowning day"—the best day they have ever known.

Chapter VIII

SHALL WE KNOW ONE ANOTHER IN HEAVEN?

There is no question connected with the future life that is more frequently and earnestly asked than, "Shall we know one another in Heaven?" The question is interesting at all times, but it becomes particularly so when loved ones are taken away and hearts are filled with sorrow. It is then the questions are asked in all sincerity, "Shall we see them again?" and, "Will those precious relationships which life has given endure?" People everywhere want to know whether in that purer, better life they will recognize those with whom they had sweet fellowship in Christian service, and be recognized by them. So intense is this yearning for recognition in the hearts of many, they feel that if they do not have this privilege, Heaven will lose much of its attractiveness for them. Some even go so far as to feel that they would almost rather be annihilated than live forever without renewing these fellowships of life. Better no future life, they say, than a life in which recognition of loved ones is denied. The very prospect of reunion after death with loved ones has sustained many through otherwise overwhelming bereavements of life.

Whether or not one shares these feelings of the utter emptiness of the future life without personal recognition, it is certain there is a longing in the bosom of every normal person for some assurance of a happy reunion and personal recognition in the land beyond this vale of tears.

When ground is sought on which to base the hope of personal recognition in Heaven, much is found to give substance to it. *First, the belief in future recognition is as universal as is the belief in immortality itself.* Wherever men entertain any belief of a future existence, there is found also a belief in some kind of recognition. This belief may be crude, even ludicrous, still it is there, and is fondly cherished, and has its influence on the life. The social instinct is so ineradicably embedded in the human heart that it recoils from the thought that personal knowledge and companionship end with the present existence. Go where one will, the desire for companionship will be found burning brightly in the bosom of all men. The ancients felt it, and cherished the hope of being gathered to their fathers. Plato recognized it, and spoke of it rather freely. Virgil recorded it. The Hindu incorporated it in his ancient creed. The Egyptians embalmed their dead in the hope of it. The Indian has ever looked forward to it as one of the assured realities of the Happy Hunting Ground. The very universality of this desire seems to be a strong presumption, if not proof, in favor of the belief that human beings will know one another in the future life. It is unthinkable that God would endow man with such a universal hope, a hope which dates back as far as human history extends, only to disappoint it.

Second, *the fact of personal identity also adds weight to the presumption of future recognition.* If individuals are to be the same persons there as they are here, the consciousness of personal identity, it would seem, would require personal recognition and fellowship. Lives are so interwoven here that the consciousness of being one's self there, it would appear, necessarily carries with it not only the memory of such relationships, but also the ability to recognize at least those who contributed so largely to such associations. How could there be any personal identity without such ability?

Third, *reason, also, would seem to teach personal recognition.* Wherein is the wisdom of creating these dear relationships, enjoining and encouraging them, even giving them the sanction of religion, if they are simply incidental and temporary? Reason appears to be well on the side of the hope of personal recognition.

Fourth, *the nature of love, likewise, argues for recognition.* No one can love another without adding something substantial and abiding to his own soul, as well as to the soul of the object of that love. Loved ones become an integral part of one's self, so much so that one is incomplete without the object of his love. Love has always been an abiding treasure of life. Paul knew this when he wrote, "And now abideth faith, hope, and love, these three; but the greatest of these is love" (I Cor. 13:13, R.V.).

Fifth, there is the implication that *people will continue to be interested in the same things there in which their hearts are most engaged here.* Of course the little details of human life which connect them with earthly surroundings will cease to interest them, because they will be no longer needed and are intended to be only temporary. But the great fundamental affairs of this life which have interested people in their souls, and for which they have labored with kindred spirits during the weary years of their earthly pilgrimage, will still be important to them. This fact seems to be brought out very clearly in the visit which Moses and Elias made to Christ on the mount of transfiguration. There these heavenly visitants talked with Him about the great atonement which He was to make—a subject in which they had been vitally interested when on earth. And now, though they have been away from earth for centuries, they have in no wise lost their interest in the great plan of redemption and its results, nor their sympathy for it. And so shall all believers be interested, as dwellers in that fair land along with their friends and loved ones, in the carrying out of God's loving purposes for which they labored here. It does not seem too much to believe that those whose chief joy here was to do His will, and whose knowledge of that will is now infinitely enlarged and purified, will be more interested in it and more conscious of their associates and fellow-laborers than they were on earth. Death, while making many changes, will not rob believers of the memory of those gloriously happy years spent in conscious, intelligent fellowship with one another, and with Him here. And it is unthinkable to believe that they will be one whit less interested in Heaven than they were here in the continuation of the work begun on earth, and in which they were permitted to share. So from these considerations it must be concluded that the inhabitants of Heaven will not know less of each other than they did here. Paul was sure that is true, for he wrote, "Now I know in part; but then I shall know even as also I am known" (I Cor. 13:12).

In studying the teaching of the Scripture in regard to the question of future recognition, it is necessary to bear in mind that there are many questions on which one would wish the clearest revelation and does not always find it; the reason for this lack is that the future life is so vastly different from the present that it is not possible to put the revelation into language which man could understand in his present state. Paul encountered this difficulty when he was caught up into the third Heaven. There he saw and heard things which it is not lawful for man to utter, or, as one popular modern translation puts it, he "heard sacred secrets which no human lips can repeat." While Paul knew what those secrets were, he could not frame them into words the dear saints at Corinth would understand. So there are many details concerning their relation to their loved ones in Heaven that Christians would like to know, but cannot because of their deficiency in language and understanding; but there are revealed great outlines of the truth sufficiently distinct to satisfy their hearts until they reach the shining shore and experience what now can only be a glorious anticipation.

What are some of the great facts unmistakably set forth in the Scripture concerning heavenly recognition? First, when the believer reaches his eternal home in the Father's house, he will be there with a new and wonderfully enlarged knowledge. "For now we see through a glass, darkly," declares the apostle, "but then face to face: now I know in part; but then shall I know even as also I am known" (I Cor. 13:12). In this life, man's intellectual and spiritual faculties are united to a body, seriously disarranged by the Fall, and impaired through sin; but when the spirit is released from this limitation, he will be able to comprehend as never before the infinite greatness and goodness of God toward the children of men. He will be given such knowledge of the wisdom of God, of His purpose in salvation, and of the mysteries of the universe, that he will be able to serve Him perfectly and without failure in the prosecution of His wonderful works of grace. Is it not logical to infer that with this marvelously increased knowledge he will there come to a better acquaintance with others than was ever known here?

Second, it is said that the names of believers are written in Heaven. "Rejoice not," said the Lord, "that the devils are subject to you, but rather rejoice because your names are written in Heaven." The name stands for the person. It means him and no one else. His name marks him as an individual distinct from all other individuals. And this Scripture, also, would seem to teach that each one is not only known, but known before he arrives. It implies that in the final gathering of "the general assembly of the church of the first-born which are written in heaven," each will know his name, and that it will be likewise known to others.

Third, the hope of mutual recognition has always belonged to the life of faith. The child of God in every age of man has cherished not only the hope of a future life, but of knowing and being known. The record concerning each of the patriarchs, Abraham, Isaac, and Jacob is that on his death he was said to be "gathered to his people." This gathering to his people would have no virtue as a hope if it did not carry with it the fact of personal recognition, for one cannot be said to be gathered to his people if he does not know them when he arrives where they are. In Matthew 22:31, 32, it is written, "As touching the resurrection of the dead, have ye not read that which was spoken unto you by God, saying, I am the God of Abraham, and the God of Isaac, and the God of Jacob? God is not the God of the dead, but of the living." One idea is quite clear from this: Abraham is still Abraham; Isaac is still Isaac; Jacob is still Jacob. Each still exists in his own identity and distinctiveness. And as such, each one is known to the other, and each one to God.

Of Moses and Aaron there was a like declaration of what was to them included in death: "Get thee up and die in the mountain whither thou goest up and be gathered to thy people." Aaron died on Mount Hor and "was gathered to his people"; but Aaron's people were not buried on Mount Hor, or near there. Aaron must have believed by this statement that upon his death he would enter into the company and companionship of those who had already departed, and with whom life would be continued. It was in the faith of seeing again his loved ones that he died on Mount Hor.

When Jacob was mourning over the loss of Joseph and refused to be comforted, his only consolation was: "I will go down into the grave unto my son mourning" (Gen. 37:35). There would be no consolation in going down into the grave to Joseph unless there were definite recognition and reunion with his beloved son. Similarly David found comfort for himself on the death of his son, for he declared, "I shall go to him, he shall not return to me." Is one not justified in concluding that since God has so faithfully and uniformly recorded these declarations, that He thereby endorses and justifies the expectation of recognition? The mere fact that these statements are recorded and allowed to stand unchallenged must mean that this is true.

Fourth, in the teaching of the Lord and His apostles, it is found that in every illustration and inference on the subject of the future life where it might be expected, recognition is either stated or assumed as a matter of course. For example, in the parable of the rich man and Lazarus it is implied that neither had any difficulty in recognizing the other though each was in marvelously changed circumstances. Lazarus was not now the beggar but the bosom friend of Abraham, one of God's princes, while the rich man was in torment. And what could have prompted the request to send Lazarus to his father's house to speak to his five brethren lest they come to that place of torment, unless there was definite recognition of Lazarus himself, and concern for his brethren who were still on earth?

Again, Paul reminds the bereaved ones at Thessalonica that sleeping saints would be raised, living ones changed, and *both* caught up together to be forever with the Lord (I Thess. 4:13-18). And he concludes, "Wherefore, comfort one another with these words." Surely the essence of the comfort of reunion would be recognition of one another.

And again, Paul describes his converts in Thessalonica as his hope, his joy, his crown in the presence of the Lord Jesus Christ at His coming (I Thess. 2:19, 20). Evidently Paul fully expected to be able to recognize these souls and to be recognized by them. For how could he rejoice in them before Christ unless he recognized them as those he loved and labored with on earth? But Paul goes further; in writing to the Corinthians he states very definitely that he fully expects mutual recognition between himself and his converts. He says, "As also ye have acknowledged us in part, that we are your rejoicing, even as ye also are ours in the day of the Lord Jesus" (II Cor. 1:14). And Paul makes definite use of this expectation, for he comforts himself in the midst of his arduous labors with the reflection that he and his Corinthian converts will rejoice in each other in the Father's house. There must be, of course, mutual recognition before there can be mutual joy.

Fifth, the Bible exemplifies recognition by presenting the Person of the resurrected Christ as the first fruits of them that sleep. He was changed after His return from the grave, but His identity was not destroyed; His name, His face, His voice, His hands to the very wound prints, were the same. Now the teaching is that as He arose, so will believers be raised also—changed and yet unchanged, glorified but still recognizable, knowing even as they are known. All this should give perfect confidence, for nothing could be more clearly or unmistakably established than the belief in future recognition.

Sixth, the Bible does more than presuppose recognition—it affirms it. On this point nothing could be surer evidence than what Christ Himself has to say about it. In the great promise given to His intimate friends in that loving talk which He had with them just before His death, He tells them quite definitely that it would be His joyous work in Heaven to make ready for them. "I go to prepare a place for you. And if I go and prepare a place for you, I will come again, and receive you unto myself; that where I am, there ye may be also" (John

14:2, 3). The last thing He would do would be to deceive these men who had followed Him in the regeneration, for He says, "If it were not so, I would have told you"; that is, if there were to be no heavenly reunion between Himself and these loving, trusting friends He would have told them. He would not have allowed them to continue hoping and wishing and dreaming that it might be so, only to disappoint them grievously at last. Christ evidently made this statement that the disciples, together with all who believe on Him through their word, might know that every word He said to them about the Father's house, and Himself going to receive them at the hour of death, could be relied upon to the fullest possible extent. How real all of this makes the other world, and how near it brings one to it!

Seventh, there is yet another consideration which lends definite force to the doctrine of mutual recognition in Heaven. It lies in the fact that believers enter Heaven not as strangers and outsiders, but as members of the family of God. It is written, "He came unto his own, and his own received him not. But as many as received him, to them gave he power [authority] to become the sons of God, even to them that believe on his name" (John 1:11, 12). And when He speaks of the Father's house as the place where all the family will be gathered, He wants His children to think of it as a home, as a family, as an abiding place, every word of which is suggestive of acquaintance, recognition, and fellowship. But, mark it, the children of God are not introduced into that family at death; they do not come into it when they are ushered into the mansions of glory, but are born into sonship the moment they believe on Christ as personal Saviour. And all who thus believe, constitute the "one family in heaven and earth." No new relation at death is formed, for they are already the sons of God, and bound together in one family. It is inconceivable, therefore, that the members of the family who are associated so intimately in the Father's house cannot recognize each other.

Dr. Charles Hodge, in his theology, has suggested that they probably err who suppose that Heaven is too radically different from life and society here. Perhaps if they could imagine a state of human society from which all evil and all that belongs to a temporal and fleshly condition are eliminated, they could get a fair mental picture of the realm of the redeemed. But the trouble is that the imagination is hardly equal to that task. People are so tied to the sinful and the fleshly and the temporal that the imagination staggers in the effort to picture a state without these things.

Eighth, the Bible teaches that one's ability to recognize others in Heaven will extend far beyond those whom he knew personally on earth. Each will be able to recognize, just how is unknown, those never seen on earth. Peter, James and John on the mount of transfiguration recognized Moses and Elias, whom they had never known in the flesh, and who had lived centuries before under entirely different circumstances; so shall all the children of God be able to recognize those of whom they have heard and read but have never seen. It is not going beyond the bounds of the Scripture to state that saints of all ages will recognize and be recognized, and learn through each other the wonderful works of God in the past; and together be taught the glory and the blessedness of the ages to come. For example, after the believer has spent a lifetime studying the Psalms, will he not be able to recognize David in Heaven, if he should be permitted to hear him repeat the Twenty-third Psalm? The heart and mind of Paul are in his Epistles, and one should have no difficulty recognizing him through them. And surely there will be no difficulty in knowing John, the beloved disciple, after having read his Epistles, and the Book of Revelation. What is true of these is true of all God's children; for yonder world is not to be peopled with thin, bodiless ghosts, but with real people, having not only the human spirit but the human form, with the limiting and hampering conditions removed to which bodily existence is subjected in this world. And the fine, unfettered freedom about the movements of our Lord during the post-resurrection period, would indicate the larger liberty and knowledge of the sons of God in the world beyond.

Not only will people know one another there, but they will know one another far more intimately and truly than they ever knew each other here. In this life, owing to the infirmities of the flesh, there are many opportunities for misunderstandings. It is easy to misinterpret the motives and purposes of very dear friends, because the full story is not known. Often opinions are formed and conclusions drawn on very partial and imperfect knowledge, and many a poor soul has suffered untold agony simply because he was misunderstood and misjudged by another.

Hannah, for example, was in deep distress of soul the day she entered the temple to lay her case before the Lord; but Eli, the high priest, misjudged her. He thought she was drunk. Here are two godly people, acting from the best motives, and under the most favorable circumstances, yet one is woefully misjudged by the other. How often is that the case in this life! But in Heaven there will be no room for misunderstanding and misjudging.

And the fact that everyone will have perfect knowledge, and thus be able to understand all others fully, opens a realm of attractive possibilities. No more will there be the weary body and the overwrought nerves to disturb the mind and wreck the judgment. The aspiring soul, no longer fretting within its narrow confines and longing for the hour of freedom, as the caged bird beats against the bars, will be released that it may exercise itself to its fullest capacity. There will be no more sickness, and weariness of toil, and crushing physical weight to bear; but in the strength of the great freedom and joy of the unfettered life, one of the richest of all the blessings to be enjoyed will be the recognition of companions in the struggles down here—those who helped in the battle through to the end.

But let it not be forgotten that after all, the chief attraction of Heaven will be the Saviour Himself. The whole life to come will center in Christ, as it ought to be centered in Him here. Believers will then hold their place in life through unnumbered and unmeasured cycles by the continued active agency of the Man Jesus. "Because I live, ye shall live also."

One of the most remarkable points in the teachings of Christ is the emphasis He places on companionship with His people, especially in the life of the world to come. To feel the force of it one has only to note such statements as these: "And where I am there shall also my servant be"; "That where I am there ye may be also." "Father, I will that they also whom thou hast given me be with me where I am, that they may behold my glory." He is evidently counting on being with His own; and His own should be counting on being with Him. The real fullness of the future life after all is life with Him who is our life.

CHAPTER IX

WHAT AND WHERE IS HEAVEN?

THUS FAR in these studies of the life of the believer after death, it has been shown from the Bible that in the Lord Jesus Christ the believer is the possessor of eternal life, and will never really die. His body will fall asleep; but he himself, his real self, his spirit goes immediately to be with Christ. But that is not all; the body is not to be discarded like a worn-out garment tossed into the discard, but will be resurrected and refashioned, not like the body that was put into the grave, but like unto the body of glory of the Son of God. And in that new body, according to the deeds done in the old body, the believer will receive his rewards at the judgment seat of Christ, and will then enter upon his final and eternal abode.

Where is this final abode to be? This is a matter about which little is known, for it is generally neglected. One seldom hears Heaven mentioned in conversation in religious circles; and even in church services it is rarely discussed. Because there is such a lack of knowledge of Heaven that people entertain a variety of opinions. Some claim there is no Heaven, declaring that all the Heaven there is, is found and enjoyed here, and not in an after life in some strange, faraway land. All teaching concerning Heaven as the future abode of men they regard as pure speculation, wild theory, or mere wishful thinking.

Others affirm that they do not know whether there is a Heaven or not. There may be one, it is possible there might be, but they do not know. They have formed no definite opinion either for or against the idea. They claim to be so busy with the affairs of life here that they have neither the time nor the opportunity to investigate the matter. And besides, they do not regard it of sufficient importance to devote much consideration to a subject about which so little can be known. They believe, they say, that if they do the best they know, when they die they will go to Heaven, if there is one; and if there is none, they will be none the worse for not bothering about it. It is to be feared there are many professing Christians who take such a position. They are willing to leave the future entirely in God's hands and go on living without troubling themselves about it. That may seem to be a wise and prudent position to take, but is it not contrary to the will of God? To refuse to consider the subject of Heaven, or to neglect to do so, is not far short of the sin of dealing deceitfully with the Word of God.

There are many, however, who are anxious to know all there is to be known of Heaven, and welcome any help to this end. They want to know not because of idle curiosity, but for the inspiration, strength, and comfort which this knowledge affords. God is evidently pleased to have His own do this; for if not, it stands to reason He would not have said so much about Heaven in His Word. The word *Heaven* occurs some five hundred and fifty times in the Scripture. Christ Himself referred to it quite frequently, declaring more than once that He came down from Heaven, and that in due time He would return thither. John, in the apocalyptic vision, was permitted to see Heaven, and that not externally only. A door was opened and he was able to behold something of the glory that is within. "After this," he writes, "I looked, and behold a door was opened in heaven," and through that door he saw "a throne" set in Heaven, and a glorious Personage seated upon it. And there was a rainbow round about that throne, in sight like unto an emerald. And he heard the worshiping throng joyfully exclaiming, "Thou art worthy, O Lord, to receive glory and honor and power: for thou hast created all things." But more marvelous still, John is invited to "Come up hither" with the promise that he would be shown things "to come hereafter" (Rev. 4:1-11). As a result of that glorious experience of John, the Church possesses today this incomparable book, "The Revelation of Jesus Christ, which God gave unto him, to show unto his servants things which must shortly come to pass," filled to overflowing with truth concerning Heaven, and interspersed with glorious word pictures of its matchless beauty and purity, its people and its praise.

But even with all this great body of revelation, when the mind enters upon an eager search for knowledge concerning the eternal home of the redeemed, it meets a most baffling and painful consciousness of being incapable of conceiving what Heaven is like, or the mode of life there. Before a thing can be revealed, there must be a language and a symbol of revelation. Before the mind can conceive and understand, there must be an essential capacity within the mind, a faculty to receive.

There is not language, there is no symbol to portray fully; and there is not sufficient capacity within man's being to receive a full understanding of what life will be in Heaven. That is one serious difficulty of understanding even the facts which God has graciously revealed concerning Heaven.

Then there is a second difficulty. Some feel they must make Heaven a strange, unreal sort of place. In their concern, for example, not to do injustice to it, they are averse to conceive of it under any aspect that has the slightest touch of the finite about it. They forget that the personal qualities that make up the human soul are the only personal qualities of which one knows anything; unless these human qualities are employed in forming a conception of Heaven, therefore, it must of necessity become an unreal and unthinkable thing. It is evident, then, that any conclusion which one forms of Heaven, so far as the general outlines are concerned, must be modeled after the scheme of life that one has already learned to know.

With this thought in mind, what are some of the facts revealed concerning Heaven which may be grasped even with the limited capacity at one's command?

First, *it is real.* It is not a matter of idle speculation, but a fact about which there can be no reasonable controversy. In the most direct and definite way imaginable the Lord gave assurance of its reality. "In my Father's house are many mansions: if it were not so, I would have told you. I go to prepare a place for you" (John 14:2). He would deal fairly with them; He always had done so; and now at the end He would not deceive them on any matter, much less on one so important to them at the time as this one. In consideration of His definite and specific assertion, there can be nothing more certain than that Heaven is real. It is not a dream, a fond, but foundationless wish; it is as He describes it. If this were not true, He would have told His faithful followers and not allowed them to spend their days in sacrifice and toil in the vain delusion that they would have a glorious home with Him in a better world.

Second, *it is not far away.* Many think it is. They sing about that faraway land of the blessed. But in reality it is not far removed from this present life. There is no great distance between that world and this one. And there is no dark, rolling stream over which the trembling soul is transported to some mysterious and dreadful shore. David, in the long ago, sang about this transition as only "the valley of the *shadow* of death," declaring that when he came to walk through it, he would "fear no evil," for the Good Shepherd would be with him, and His rod and staff would comfort and sustain him. And does not the Psalmist's conception of death harmonize perfectly with Christ's statement to the penitent thief, when He said to him, "Today shalt thou be with me in paradise" (Luke 23:43)? There was to be no long, painful voyage; but they would be in paradise before their blood congealed at the foot of their crosses. It is not far away, for to be absent from the body is to be present with the Lord.

Third, *it is a state of permanency.* That does not mean fixation or stagnation, but freedom from all anxiety of change or defeat. The inhabitants of the holy city are blessed with a sense of infinite protection and repose. They have come into an existence where no hope is frustrated, no plan is ever broken, and no task remains unfinished. They are where the limitations of earth, the checks and hindrances of failing time, and disease, and weakness, and death are unknown, and where every hope and plan conceived will find complete fulfillment. This is the promise voiced by the apostle Paul when he said, "We know that . . . we have a building of God, an house not made with hands, eternal in the heavens" (II Cor. 5:1). That is sure.

Fourth, *it is a definite location.* There are those who argue that Heaven is merely a state or condition of the mind. They even go so far as to say that to insist on Heaven being a place is to show a woeful lack of an understanding and appreciation of spiritual affairs. To be sure there is a state or condition involved, but that does not prove there is no such thing as a place, nor does it in the least conflict with it. Indeed, the one implies the other; for of what value is a state or condition without a place in which to exercise it? A right state is a preparation for the right place. Abraham's bosom suggests a place. Paradise, to which Christ went accompanied by the penitent thief, certainly denotes a place. Our Lord calls it a place, "I go to prepare a place for you." He most certainly gave the impression to His disciples that He meant for them to understand that it was a definite place, a real location, rather than a mere state or condition of the mind.

Not only does He speak most definitely of Heaven as a place, but He taught His disciples when they pray to say, "Our Father, which art in heaven" (Matt. 6:19, 20). The word Heaven is used in a variety of meanings both in the Old and New Testaments, but the chief are these: (1) the dwelling-place of God; (2) the abode from which Jesus Christ came, and to which He has returned; and (3) the destination of the perfected saints. It is to be noted that in all three senses the idea of a definite place prevails beyond the peradventure of a doubt. Then, again, He urges the believer to lay up treasures in Heaven, "where neither moth nor rust doth corrupt, and where thieves do not break through nor steal" (Matt. 6:20). Moth and rust do not operate in a state or condition, nor do thieves break through and steal in such an intangible situation. If language is to be allowed to convey thought, it must follow that a place is meant.

Again, Heaven is spoken of as the "Father's house." A house is real and brings to us all the precious intimacies of fellowship in a definite location. Heaven is also frequently referred to as the heavenly city of the Old Testament worthies. "These all died in faith, not having received the promises, but having seen them afar off, and were persuaded of them, and embraced them, and confessed that they were strangers and pilgrims on the earth"; and the inspired comment is, "they that say such things declare plainly that they seek a country." And it is further stated by way of explanation, "if they had been mindful of that country from whence they came out, they might have had opportunity to have returned. But now they desire a better country, that is, an heavenly: wherefore God is not ashamed to be called their God: for *he hath prepared for them a city*" (Heb. 11:13-16).

The city which God has prepared for those who are strangers and pilgrims on earth because of their devotion to Him, is firmly founded; its builder and maker is God. Man's cities do not continue; they rise on a cursed earth and soon crumble into dust. Here "we" have no continuing city, "we" seek one to come (Heb. 13:14). And the name of the city is given; it is called "the heavenly Jerusalem" (Heb. 12:22). The earthly Jerusalem was a real city in a definite location, and so must the heavenly Jerusalem be.

Paul relates how he himself was caught up to the third Heaven (II Cor. 12:2), which must imply that he found himself in as definite a location as he had ever been in.

It is inconceivable how one can be just and fair to God's infallible Word and to the faith of the saints of all ages, and not believe that the Scripture refers not to an idea or fantastic city, but to a true, real, God-built city, substantial and eternal and located in a definite place in God's infinite universe.

Since it is a place, what kind of place is it?

First, *it is a place of ideal order and government.* John in his vision of Heaven, when the door was opened and he was permitted to see within, noticed among other things "a throne set in heaven, and one sat on the throne" (Rev. 4:2). "Throne" denotes the seat of authority and regulated government. Heaven has a throne, and therefore is a place of perfect rule, of harmonious blessedness and abiding security. Christ had reference to this government when He taught His disciples to pray, "Thy will be done in earth, as it is in heaven" (Matt. 6:10).

Second, *it is commodious.* One of the objections sometimes urged against Heaven is lack of space to accommodate the vast number of people who are supposed to have their habitation in the Holy City. From the death of righteous Abel down to the death of the one a moment ago, uncounted millions have fallen asleep in the hope of a blessed immortality, and to give them all a place would require enormous space. But God is never embarrassed for want of space. He has room enough and to spare for any requirement.

John, in the Book of Revelation, gives the dimensions of the Holy City. It is fifteen hundred miles square—a perfect cube. That means it is as far as from Maine to Florida, and from the Atlantic ocean to half way across the continent, and an equal distance from top to bottom. Consider the significance of these distances. Someone has calculated that if the world stood as it is for a hundred thousand years, and a billion people died in each generation, there would be ample space for all in Heaven. Allowing fifteen feet to the story, the city would be five hundred and twenty-eight thousand stories high. Every one of the stories would contain two million, two hundred and fifty thousand square miles, according to this mathematician; and all the stories combined would total one trillion, one hundred and eighty-eight billion square miles. It is utterly impossible to conceive the immensity of the city.

Earth's present population is around two billions. In the six thousand years since Adam and Eve were created there have been one hundred and eighty generations, allowing thirty-three and one-third years to the generation. Now, says the mathematician, supposing every generation were as large as the present (of course it was not), three hundred and sixty billions would be the total population of earth since the creation of man.

Dividing these billions into families of five to a family, there would be seventy-two billion families; and then dividing the number of families into the number of square miles, there would be for every family an area of sixteen and one-half square miles; room for mansions, walks, driveways, fields, forest, orchard and gardens, lakes and streams—everything that heart could wish. This distribution of space is on the assumption that every generation were as large as the present one, and all were saved and safe within the jasper walls. In that event there would be for every family of five, sixteen and one-half square miles, or three and three-tenths square miles for every man, woman, and child that has ever lived.

The Department of Eugenics of the Carnegie Institute has estimated the total population of the world since man first appeared on the earth at thirty billions. On this estimate of population there would be an area of one hundred and ninety-eight miles for every family, or thirty-nine and three-fifths square miles for every m[illegible]n, woman and child from Adam to the present time. [illegible]

These estimates as to space and population g[illegible] ma[illegible] idea of the size and possible number of inhabitants Heaven can accommodate. And there is every reason to believe there will be no waste space there; that each mansion, each place prepared will be filled.

Third, *it is a place of beauty.* God loves the beautiful or He would not have put so much beauty in this world. Heaven is beautiful beyond comparison. The Bible does not go into details, but it tells us enough to let us know that beauty in Heaven has reached perfection. The beauty of earth fades into insignificance in comparison with the beauty of Heaven. John caught a glimpse of it and tried to describe something of its beauty. But the best he could do was to use a few familiar symbols such as: "The walls are jasper, the foundations garnished with precious stones, and every gate a pearl, and the city is of pure gold like unto clear glass."

A little girl was born blind, it is said, and a great doctor was able to give her sight. The little girl was amazed at the beauty of the world, and exclaimed, "Oh, Mamma, why did you not tell me how beautiful it was?" And the mother wiped her tears of joy away and said, "My precious child, I tried to tell you but I could not do so." Some day the redeemed will probably say to John, "John, why did you not tell us how beautiful Heaven is?" And John will say, "I tried to tell you; I wrote the twenty-first and twenty-second chapters of Revelation to let you know something of it, but I could not tell you fully."

Fourth, *it is a place of perfect service*. Since Heaven is where God's will is fully done—then it must be a place of perfect service. There is much in the Scripture that would indicate there will be most congenial and delightful service for the redeemed. In his description of Heaven, John says, "And there shall be no more curse: but the throne of God and of the Lamb shall be in it; and his servants shall serve him" (Rev. 22:3). To be sure, Heaven is a place of perfect rest, not the rest of inactivity, but of perfect satisfaction in activity. What kind of activity? For one thing, there will be *intellectual activity*. Heaven is a place of never tiring thought. No stagnation can be there. What marvelous things shall the redeemed come to know there? There were many things they wanted to know here, and the problems were too high for them to understand; but in Heaven, where every faculty will be quickened and intensified, and all the pages of knowledge unfolded before their wondering and admiring eyes, they shall have complete understanding of every problem and every question will be answered. "For now we see through a glass, darkly; but then face to face: now I know in part; but then shall I know even as also I am known" (I Cor. 13:12).

Then in Heaven, too, there will be congenial *social activity*. There is nothing more delightful here than human association. Man is not normally a solitary creature, preferring to be alone. He craves companionship. He was not created to live alone. He must have congenial associates to be his best self. In Heaven the saints enter into a delightful association. There will be no gossip, no backbiting, no meddling. The Devil will not be there, nor any who follow his ways. The lewd, the vulgar, the obscene, the liar, the slanderer, the mean and contemptible will all be excluded. "And there shall in no wise enter into it anything that defileth, neither whatsoever worketh abomination, or maketh a lie: but they which are written in the Lamb's book of life" (Rev. 21:27). There will be no friction, no misunderstanding, but perfect appreciation; a perfect environment with perfect people in it will constitute the social life of Heaven.

What high and ennobling association! "And I say unto you, That many shall come from the east and west, and shall sit down with Abraham, and Isaac, and Jacob, in the kingdom of heaven" (Matt. 8:11).

Fifth, *it is a place of open vision*. Here the child of God walks by faith; there the glory-vision shall be his, and he shall gaze directly upon the countenance of his blessed Lord (Rev. 22:4). Dimly now he traces the dark outlines of heavenly things, seeing through a glass darkly, but then face to fac now knowing in part, then fully. What marvelous visions await the believer!

Sixth, *it is a place of unhindered worship*. John saw the worshiping throng before the throne. On earth worshipers gather in small groups amid much weakness, and the feebleness of their praise is painfully obvious. They could not hope for its acceptance save for their Great High Priest who ever liveth to make intercession for them. Here the heart lags, the mind is dull, memory weak, and the distractions of the earthly lot obtrude unasked upon the holiest moments. Jarring notes spoil the praise, and coldness of spirit chill the thanksgiving. It is only His matchless grace that encourages the believer to know that his poor worship is accepted. But in Heaven how different it will be! What glorious unison of full-hearted, pure, untainted, and unceasing worship the redeemed shall be able to render, as they sing the song of Moses and the Lamb!

Seventh, *it is home*. The eternal, the abiding home! Christ described it as "my Father's house." A father's house is also the children's house. Home is one of the tenderest words in human language. What joyous associations are connected with it! Every true heart turns home when the day is over and the tasks are done. Kindred souls are there; loved ones are there. Home is the scene of parental and filial affection, family life and friendships. That is Heaven–at home with the Lord. Gather up all the word *home* means here, multiply it a million times and that will give you some faint idea of what Heaven is to every weary, homesick child of God. Heaven is home. When Christ referred to Heaven as the place of "many mansions" He was not thinking so much of luxury as of a suitable dwelling place, of an abode wisely planned and furnished for the comfort of the children when they arrive. Being fully acquainted with human griefs and necessities, He is fitting a place exactly suited for each one. He knows the tastes, capabilities, and attainments of believers and He has set apart a place for each one according to his need, and holds it for him. The word *home* that has meant so much here is to mean even more over there. It is Heaven.

> What joys are lost, what hopes are given,
> As through this death-struck world we roam.
> We think awhile that home is Heaven;
> We learn at length that Heaven is Home.

CHAPTER X

HOW ARE WE FITTED FOR HEAVEN?

HAVING CONSIDERED BRIEFLY the entrancing beauty and holiness of the eternal home of the redeemed, the next thing in order will be to ascertain the requirement for a place as a dweller there. It is clear that nothing that is at all incompatible with the purity and holiness of that habitation can enter it. The inhabitants are not a people, brought there indiscriminately as if by chance, or by other devious ways. Nothing that is ungodly or impure shall ever be found there. "And there shall in no wise enter into it anything that defileth, neither whatsoever worketh abomination, or maketh a lie: but they which are written in the Lamb's book of life" (Rev. 21:27).

With such qualifications required, how can anyone become fit for such a place? The question is an overwhelming one. How can any mortal man, with his old nature still clinging to him, ever feel that he is fit for Heaven, where the four living creatures "rest not day and night, saying, Holy, holy, holy, Lord God Almighty, which was, and is, and is to come" (Rev. 4:8)?

And yet it must be possible for men somehow to be

"made meet to be partakers of the inheritance of the saints in light" (Col. 1:12), for Heaven is peopled by those who have come from every nation and kindred and tongue on earth. It is certain no one can go to join the happy throng without due fitness—without something fundamental being done in him or for him, or both.

And there is another fact which adds to the difficulty of the situation. The Scripture tells of men being admitted to Heaven who appear to have no fitness for it. Take Moses, for example, who is so signally honored in Heaven that the redeemed are said to sing the song of Moses and the Lamb, thus having his name coupled with that of the Son of God in the songs of praise of the redeemed in Heaven. Moses was a great and good man in many respects, yet his life was far from correct. Because of sin God could not permit him to enter the Promised Land, even after he had led the children of Israel for forty years through all that great and terrible wilderness journey. And yet Moses is in Heaven, for he appeared "in glory" as he talked with Jesus on the mount of transfiguration of His "decease which he should accomplish at Jerusalem" (Luke 9:30, 31).

To the penitent on the cross beside Him, Christ said, "Today shalt thou be with me in paradise" (Luke 23:43). Who was this man and what was his history? He was a thief and had a long record of crimes to his credit. He was so bad he had been arrested and condemned to death for his misdoing. His record is very black even at the time those words were spoken. There is no time for him to make preparation now, for his life is fast ebbing away. He is not in position to receive any of the rites of religion. And for every good deed he has ever performed, he has dozens of bad ones to account for. Yet Christ, the pure and holy One, the God-Man, tells the dying thief that He will take him along with Him to paradise before the day is over. And the Lord never promised a poor, trusting soul anything which He did not do. How could such a one be made ready for Heaven in so brief time and under such distressing circumstances?

In the Epistle to the Colossians, Paul sets forth both the believer's inheritance and his fitness for it as clearly as is to be found anywhere in the Scripture. In the first chapter there is a very long sentence beginning with verse nine and ending with verse seventeen, and in the very center of this extended sentence are these words: "Giving thanks unto the Father, which hath made us meet to be partakers of the inheritance of the saints in light: who hath delivered us from the power of darkness, and hath translated us into the kingdom of his dear Son: in whom we have redemption through his blood, even the forgiveness of sins."

Who were these Colossians of whom such wonderful things could be said? They were a group of people who had recently been gathered together from paganism through the preaching of the Gospel. The great majority of them were no doubt Gentiles, and as such were "aliens from the commonwealth of Israel, and strangers from the covenants of promise, having no hope, and without God in the world" (Eph. 2:12): "dead in trespasses and sin," and "walking according to the course of this world."

But a radical change had been wrought in them. They are no longer "aliens and strangers" to the things of God, but have been made meet to be partakers of the inheritance of the saints in light; they have been delivered from the power of darkness and translated into the kingdom of God's dear Son.

Let it be observed that the Colossians are in possession of this meetness now. They are not hoping to be made so, but *are* already prepared for their place in Heaven.

How did these Colossians receive this fitness? If the secret of their acceptance can be discovered, then the answer to the question of fitness for Heaven is found.

There is a word used in this Scripture which furnishes the clue to the answer. It is the word "inheritance." An inheritance is an apportioned possesssion allotted to one on the basis of heirship—something which becomes his by virtue of his connection with the one who bestows it. Peter describes this remarkable inheritance more fully in his first Epistle. "Blessed be the God and Father of our Lord Jesus Christ, which according to his abundant mercy hath begotten us again unto a lively hope by the resurrection of Jesus Christ from the dead, to an inheritance incorruptible, and undefiled, and that fadeth not away, reserved in heaven for you, who are kept by the power of God through faith unto salvation ready to be revealed in the last time" (I Peter 1:3-5). What a wonderful inheritance! It is *incorruptible*. In this life everything is tending to decay and corruption. Kingdoms, empires, cities, monuments, the proudest and most massive and substantial things ever erected by man, crumble and cease to be. Even the temple, the ark, the golden cherubim, the rod of Aaron that budded, the very stones on which Jehovah engraved His Law have all disappeared. But this holy "inheritance of the saints in light" abides incorrupted and incorruptible.

The inheritance also is *undefiled.* There is nothing on earth that is unmarred by imperfection or untainted by impurities. The most beautiful and delightfully fragrant flowers are not without their poison, and there is not a scene of loveliness on earth but the trail and slime of the old serpent are all over it. But not so with the inheritance of the saints. There is not the least suggestion of defilement on it.

Nor will it *fade away.* All earthly possessions and glories fade, but the inheritance remains forever the same, for it is reserved in Heaven for those who are the heirs of it. It is safe from all possibility of depreciation or damage for it is inaccessible to accident, to foe, to thief, or to moth or rust. It was prepared from the foundation of the world and laid up in Heaven in absolute safety and perfection for those who will be heirs of it.

It is the inheritance of the *saints.* None but the blood-bought children of God can ever have part in it. It is reserved exclusively for the saints *in light,* that is to say, for saints revealed, manifested, shown as saints. Saints are in light now and walk in light, but their life is hid with Christ in God; they are yet to be made manifest, and when they are manifested it will be in the likeness of Christ, with whom they are joint-heirs. Hence the inheritance is the possession of the saints resurrected, glorified, and in their immortal state.

In view of the purity and perfection of the inheritance, the wonder grows as to how anyone can ever be qualified to come into possession of it. But that there are multitudes of poor, frail human beings fitted for it and kept securely for it, cannot be doubted.

How is this fitness secured? As Adam through his sin

drew down into his fallen and ruined state the old creation of which he was the ruler and head, so Christ, the last Adam, through His atoning sacrifice brings back all who receive Him into fellowship with God and into eternal life, and thus they become sons of God and joint-heirs with Christ Jesus to this glorious inheritance of the saints. To be sure, the heir is now a minor, under tutors and governors, but though a minor he is no less an heir. This grand estate, therefore, is the patrimony of faith. It is not the pay of a servant, but the inheritance of the child.

But who makes one fit for this inheritance? Does he do it himself, or does another do it for him? Or does he do part and someone else the remainder, and thus by both working together the fitness is finally secured? Many think this fitness depends entirely on what they do themselves. But according to the teaching of the Scripture, one's qualification for entering Heaven—his right to become partaker of this inheritance which belongs only to the saints in light—is not secured by anything which he may be able to do for himself. What could the dying thief on the cross do, for example, which would admit him into paradise?

To be sure the kind of reward one will have in Heaven, and in that sense the kind of Heaven he will be able to enjoy after reaching there, depends on the character of the deeds done in the body while on earth. But the point here is, so far as one's admittance into Heaven and his fitness to be there are concerned, there is not one single thing he can do. The Scripture very definitely teaches that one in Heaven will be no more saved than another in so far as admission is concerned. But there will be those there who will not have stored up any treasures in Heaven, and hence have no reward. All their works are burned up, but they are themselves saved, "yet so as by fire" (I Cor. 3:15). They are saved, but certainly not by anything they did, for all their works are burned. But the subject for discussion here is not rewards, but fitness to enter Heaven. And that fitness one does not provide for himself.

Does one's fitness, then, depend partly on what he does and partly on what Christ does for him? Probably a majority of professing Christians think this is the way fitness is secured. They suppose that Christ provides some of it for them, and they add the balance if they work long enough and hard enough at the task. In that case, in the last analysis, the fitness really depends on what they do for themselves. Is that idea according to the teaching of God's Word? Ask the next ten professing Christians you meet and see what they say. In all probability they will agree that the statement is correct. It is well-known that people generally think that fitness for the future life is due to some gradual improvement during life, or to some sudden change at death; while others expect a process of purification to be effected in another world.

Despite all opinions and views to the contrary, there is only one thing—no more and no less—that makes one qualified to enter Heaven; and that one thing is the atoning work of the Lord Jesus Christ. One's fitness depends not on what he has done, but solely on what Christ has done. There is just one thing that separates man from God, and that is *sin*. Remove that, and there is nothing between any soul and God. Before sin entered, man was in direct and intimate communion and fellowship with

God. But when he sinned he lost it all and was banished from the presence of God. There is only one way back to God, and that is by the removal of sin. This could be done only by Christ "who his own self bare our sins in his own body on the tree, that we, being dead to sins, should live unto righteousness" (I Peter 2:24). It was in the bearing of the awful weight of sin that Christ was heard to cry in agony of soul, "My God, my God, why hast thou forsaken me?" But whose sin was it that caused this cry of separation? It was not His sins, because He knew no sin of His own; but He was bearing "our sins in his own body" that we, being dead to sin, should "be made partakers of his holiness." When God struck at sin, the blow fell on Him because He stood for man. The *full* penalty of sin was visited on Him, not a portion of it. And since He paid that, all who believe on Him are freed from the condemnation of sin. This freedom is theirs for the taking; they do not earn it; "for the wages of sin is death; but the gift of God is eternal life through Jesus Christ our Lord" (Rom. 6:23).

But that is not all. He offers not only forgiveness of sin, but righteousness to all who will accept it. "For by one offering he hath perfected forever them that are sanctified. Whereof the Holy Ghost also is a witness to us: for after that he had said before, This is the covenant that I will make with them after those days, saith the Lord, I will put my laws into their hearts, and in their minds will I write them; and their sins and iniquities will I remember no more. Now where remission of these is, there is no more offering for sin" (Heb. 10:14-18). The believer is made perfect in Him and by Him. Now can anything be added to what He has perfected, and, as He says, perfected *forever?*

What are some of the things which Christ bestows on the believer now in the way of fitness for Heaven? First, he has *peace with God.* "Therefore being justified by faith, we have peace with God through our Lord Jesus Christ" (Rom. 5:1). What can be more reassuring than peace with God? And that peace is based solely upon the precious blood of Christ.

Second, the believer is *sanctified.* After exhorting the Corinthians to flee all sinful lusts, Paul reminds them that some of them had lived very sinful lives, "but," he hastens to add, "ye are washed, but ye are sanctified, but ye are justified in the name of the Lord Jesus, and by the Spirit of our God" (I Cor. 6:11). What God has cleansed is not to be called common or unclean; for what God does, He does perfectly. Nothing that is unclean is fit for Heaven, but since the believer is washed and sanctified by the Holy Spirit Himself, he is prepared to enter.

Third, the believer is *reconciled* to God. No one is fit for Heaven until this reconciliation is effected. Man cannot do it himself; it is done only through the sacrifice of Christ and is received by faith alone. "You, that were sometime alienated and enemies in your mind by wicked works, yet now hath he reconciled in the body of his flesh through death, to present you holy and unblamable and unreprovable in his sight" (Col. 1:21, 22).

Fourth, man's *bondage to Satan is broken.* As long as this bondage continues he is in no wise fit for Heaven. But how can it be broken? Man cannot do it, for he is the servant of Satan. There is only One who can, and

He will break it for everyone who trusts in Him. "Giving thanks unto the Father, which hath made us meet to be partakers of the inheritance of the saints in light: who hath delivered us from the power of darkness, and hath translated us into the kingdom of his dear Son: in whom we have redemption through his blood, even the forgiveness of sins" (Col. 1:12-14). The power of darkness is broken and the transfer is complete, and the believer is no longer in bondage to the god of this world. What wonderful fitness because of His grace!

When is this fitness secured? Is it a process or an act? Of some devoted and aged saint, as he is about to slip over into the celestial city, it is said, "He is surely fit for Heaven," meaning that he has at last reached the place where he is somehow qualified to enter Heaven. But did it take a long lifetime for him to become fit for Heaven? If it did, then the thief must have been an exception; or did he not reach paradise at all? No; it did not take a lifetime to make the aged saint fit to enter Heaven. Of course Heaven will be richer to him for the loving service he rendered during that long life as a Christian; but he was fit for Heaven the moment he believed. Not by a long process, but by one definite act God translates the believer *out* of the power of darkness in which the whole world lieth, and instantly translates him *into* the kingdom of the Son of His love!

What is one to do to become fit for Heaven? Just one thing—"The word is nigh thee, even in thy mouth, and in thy heart . . . that if thou shalt confess with thy mouth the Lord Jesus, and shalt believe in thine heart that God hath raised him from the dead, thou shalt be saved. For with the heart man believeth unto righteousness; and with the mouth confession is made unto salvation" (Rom. 10:8-10). Christ alone provides the fitness, and the believer has only to accept it.